Interventions for In-School Suspension

by Catherine H. Pardue, M.Ed., LPC

Reproducible Activities

Worksheets

Lessons

GRADES 4-12

Cover Design by Amy Rule
Layout by Tonya Daugherty
Edited by Susan Bowman

ISBN
1-59850-001-5

Library of Congress
Control Number:
2005929936

10 9 8 7 6
Printed in the United States

PO Box 115 • Chapin, SC 29036
(800) 209-9774 • (803) 345-1070 • Fax (803) 345-0888
yl@youthlightbooks.com • www.youthlight.com

DEDICATION

This publication is dedicated to my husband who

has always believed in me and to my children who are

my love and joy. Without the gifts from my heavenly

Father, the ability to serve students would not be

present. The love shared as a family has provided

me with a foundation to continue to learn, grow and

further develop the gifts that God has given me.

ACKNOWLEDGEMENTS

Mrs. Virginia Culbertson, principal of Merriwether Middle School, has a sincere desire to see students treated with compassion and dignity as they learn. Her philosophy, "We teach through everything we do," provides a foundation for professionals to model. It is hoped that her spirit of caring is reflected in these lessons.

Mrs. Mindy Clark, teacher of our gifted and talented students, graciously agreed to proofread this publication.

I am deeply grateful to my students, for whom I have a sincere desire to see make steps toward positive change. I am appreciative of the opportunity YouthLight, Inc. has given me, and its trust in my abilities.

TABLE OF CONTENTS

LESSON 1
ASSIGNMENT: IN-SCHOOL SUSPENSION

LESSON 2
DECISION-MAKING

LESSON 4
BUS INFRACTIONS
Timetables

INTRODUCTION

ADMINISTRATOR:

With an ever-increasing need to focus on accountability, it behooves administrators to offer students, assigned to In-School Suspension, an opportunity to correct misbehavior in hopes of maximizing learning.

The goals of this program are to positively impact change by instructing students about their behavior, providing activities for them to understand the behaviors and giving them steps to improve. Contracts are provided for students to enter into with members of administration, if the administrator deems this necessary.

Seven lessons are provided to implement as part of your school's In-School Suspension program for students in grades 4-6, 7-9 and 10-12.

Lesson 1: Assignment: In-School Suspension
Lesson 2: Decision-Making
Lesson 3: Bullying
Lesson 4: Bus Infraction
Lesson 5: Classroom and School Disruptions
Lesson 6: Conflict Resolution
Lesson 7: Organization and Study Skills

Upon administrative assignment to in-school suspension, each student completes lessons 1 and 2. **Lesson 1:** Assignment: In-School Suspension outlines corrective actions that administrators may take. **Lesson 2:** Decision-Making gives the student information on good decision-making.

If a student is placed on probation, assigned to alternative school or moved toward expulsion; the completed work documents your staffs' efforts to further assist the student in correcting the inappropriate behavior.

STUDENT:

The student has the opportunity to:
- Provide information about him/herself to your counselor and/or teachers.
- Learn about his/her behavior.
- Complete activities relevant to the misbehavior.
- Learn steps to improve.
- Enter into a contract to commit to improve his/her behavior.

PARENTS:

A parent letter is enclosed. Administrators may route this to the parent to let them know about this positive instructional program.

COUNSELOR:

Using the ISS Student Information Sheet, the counselor may consider:
- Referring the student for screening for possible learning problems, physical or emotional concerns.
- Becoming more aware of a student's home environment.
- Counseling may be needed.

TEACHERS:

At the counselor's discretion, the teacher(s) may receive input through the Teacher Contact Sheet. The information may give the teacher or team of teachers needed insight to possibly:
- Refer the student for screening for possible learning problems.
- Provide additional instructional support.
- Be more sensitive to this student's needs.
- Become more aware of this student's home environment.

HOW TO USE THIS PROGRAM

ADMINISTRATOR:

1) A parent letter is provided so administrators may notify parents of a student's assignment to this program.

2) Administrators assign the lessons to be completed on the ISS Internal Routing Sheet. This information is routed to the ISS Proctor.

3) If the administrator indicates a contract is to be completed, the ISS proctor will have the student complete it. Then the contract will be forwarded to the administrator for follow through.

ISS PROCTOR WILL:

1) Review the ISS Internal Routing Sheet and duplicate lessons 1 and 2 along with other assigned lessons.

2) Complete the ISS Maintenance Sheet by entering requested information.

3) Have the student complete the ISS Student Information Sheet, a student intake sheet. The proctor will complete the ISS Teacher Contact Sheet and route both forms to the counselor. The proctor needs to ensure the student is taking the work seriously as the worksheets can be used as documentation.

4) Establish a folder for each student. Completed work is placed in this folder.

5) Ensure the student retains the Keeper Sheet upon his/her completion of the lesson.

6) Have the student complete the Contract if indicated on the ISS Internal Routing Sheet. If completed, the Contract will be routed to the administrator for follow through.

COUNSELOR WILL:

1) Review the ISS Student Information Sheet to consider possible interventions.

2) Route the ISS Teacher Contact Sheet to the student's teachers if needed.

3) Meet with the student if needed.

Date _____

Student's Name _____

Dear Parent:

Your child is being assigned to our In-School Suspension Program. In an effort to assist your child with the behavior he/she demonstrated; your child will be working on the lessons marked below from **Interventions for In-School Suspension** by Catherine H. Pardue.

The goal of this program is to positively impact change by instructing students about their behavior, giving them activities to understand their behaviors and giving them steps to improve. Contracts are provided for students to enter into with members of administration, if the administrator finds this is necessary.

Date of Infraction _____

Disciplinary Infraction _____

✔ Assignment: In-School Suspension   ❑ Classroom and School Disruptions

✔ Decision-Making   ❑ Conflicts and Resolutions

❑ Bullying   ❑ Organization and Study Skills

❑ Bus Infractions

We hope you will talk to your child and ask him/her about what has been learned.

If you have any questions, please contact me at: _____.

Sincerely,

Principal

ISS INTERNAL ROUTING SHEET

(**Principal:** Enter requested data and route this sheet to your ISS Proctor at least one day prior to the student's entry. This will allow time for the proctor to reproduce the assigned lessons.)

_____

Date   **Student's First and Last Name**

Circle the appropriate grade level: 4   5   6   7   8   9   10   11   12

ISS Proctor: This student is to complete the lessons as indicated:

✔ Lesson 1: Assignment – In-School Suspension

✔ Lesson 2: Decision-Making

❑ Lesson 3: Bullying*

❑ Lesson 4: Bus Infraction*

❑ Lesson 5: Classroom and School Disruptions*

❑ Lesson 6: Conflicts and Resolution*

❑ Lesson 7: Organization and Study Skills*

❑ Contract: Student should complete the contract for this lesson.

Contract is available for this lesson.

Comments:

_____

_____

_____

_____

_____

_____

_____

_____

_____

Administrator's Signature   **Date**

INSTRUCTIONS FOR ISS PROCTOR

General Information

1) Complete the ISS Student Maintenance Sheet. Be sure to indicate the name of the activity the student completes for lessons 3-7.

2) Duplicate lessons one, two and the administrator-assigned lessons indicated on the ISS Internal Routing Sheet. Timetables are provided at the beginning of each lesson. Pens or pencils are needed.

   Example: Jane disrupts the bus in grades 6, 7 and 8. Therefore, the lessons and activities would be as shown below.

Grade	Lessons	Sections	Activity
6	Assignment In-School Suspension	1, 2	None
6	Decision-Making	1, 2	Lunch Menu
6	Bus Infraction	1, 2, 3	Alisha's Hurt Feelings
7	Assignment In-School Suspension	1, 2	None
7	Decision-Making	1, 2	Matching: Decisions with Consequences
7	Bus Infraction	1, 2, 3	Good and Bad Choices
8	Assignment In-School Suspension	1, 2	None
8	Decision-Making	1, 2	Good and Bad Decisions
8	Bus Infraction	1, 2, 3	The Group

3) Each student will read all sections of each lesson. Then each student will complete only one of the activities in lessons 3-7. There are three activities for each grade level. It is imperative that you record which lesson is assigned for that date. This is necessary because if the student is reassigned for the same lesson either during this year or another year, the student is to be given another activity.

   Note: In Lesson 7: Organization and Study Skills, for grades 7-9 and 10-12, the student will complete sections 1, 2 and 3 and one of the three Read It activities.

4) On the ISS Teacher Contact Sheet, complete the information requested. Then attach it to the ISS Student Information Sheet and route both forms to the counselor.

5) The Keeper Sheet lists Steps to Improve. Give this to the student to take home.

6) Contracts are provided at the end of lessons 3-7. If the Contract box of the ISS Internal Routing Sheet is marked, have the student complete the contract. Then route the contract to the principal.

7) Make a folder for each student and file the completed activities and sections.

8) On the timetables for each lesson, Total time represents the estimated amount of time needed for the student to complete the required sections and the activity that you assign on that date.

ISS STUDENT MAINTENANCE SHEET

Record the information requested. In the **Other** column, record the additional lesson number, if assigned. In the **Name of Activity** column, record the title of the activity you give to the student to complete with the sections. The first two lines are given as examples for you to follow.

School's Name

Date	Name	Grade	L1	L2	Other	Name of Activity
3/15/10	Sample, Katrina	6	✔	✔	L4	Alisha's Hurt Feelings
1/7/11	Sample, Katrina	7	✔	✔	L7	My Favorite Treat

LESSON 1
ASSIGNMENT: IN-SCHOOL SUSPENSION

Grades 4-6 & Grades 7-12

SECTION 1:
WHY AM I HERE?

Directions:

1) Print your first and last name and date on the spaces provided.

_____

      Student's Name   **Date**

2) Read the information below.

Do you know why you were placed in In-School Suspension?

Do you know why acting badly is harmful to you and others?

- How you act in school is important. When you act badly, you will not learn as much.

- When you misbehave or act out, you may not hear what your teacher is saying.

- When you act badly, you keep other students from learning. You are disrupting class.

3) On the next page, you will find some reasons why students do not behave in school.

ISS STUDENT INFORMATION SHEET

Directions:

1) Print your first and last name and date on the spaces provided.

_____

      Student's Name   **Date**

2) Mark any item that might be causing you a problem or causing you to act up.
   Note: Your counselor will receive a copy of this sheet and may share it with your teachers to help you.

HOME AND FAMILY

❑ I have problems at home with my brothers or sisters.
❑ I have problems at home with the person who takes care of me.
❑ I have problems studying at home.
❑ I have problems with my mom's boyfriend.
❑ I have problems with my father's girlfriend.
❑ I have problems with my dad.
❑ I have problems with my mom.
❑ Other: _____
   _____
   _____

SCHOOL / CLASSROOM

❑ I have trouble reading.
❑ I don't understand what I read.
❑ I have trouble with math.
❑ I have trouble remembering what I learn.
❑ I am being bullied.
❑ I can't concentrate.
❑ I cheat sometimes.
❑ Other: _____
   _____
   _____

PHYSICAL / ENVIRONMENTAL CONCERNS

❑ I have trouble hearing.
❑ I have trouble seeing.
❑ I have trouble with my speech.
❑ I daydream a lot.
❑ I can't sit still.
❑ I have trouble paying attention.
❑ I get angry or mad at school.
❑ The lights bother me.
❑ I have trouble breathing.
❑ I feel sad.
❑ I feel like crying.
❑ I am trying to fit in.
❑ I need a friend.
❑ I am trying to be cool.
❑ Other students are mad at me.
❑ Other students bother me.
❑ Other: _____
   _____
   _____

ISS TEACHER CONTACT SHEET

ISS Proctor: Complete this sheet by filling in the student's name and date of assignment to ISS. Place a check mark by the lesson(s) the student completed today. Attach this to the ISS Student Information Sheet and route both to the counselor.

Student's Name   **Date**

This student was assigned to In-School Suspension on the date given. The principal assigned the lessons marked below along with Assignment: In-School Suspension and Decision-Making.

- ✔ Assignment – In-School Suspension
- ✔ Decision-Making
- ❑ Bullying
- ❑ Bus Infraction
- ❑ Classroom and School Disruptions

- ❑ Conflicts and Resolution
- ❑ Organization and Study Skills

These lessons provided the student with the following:

- Opportunity to give information about concerns he/she may have.
- Disciplinary steps an administrator might take.
- Information specific to his/her behavior
- Activities relevant to the behavior
- Steps to Improve
- Contract was available if administratively requested.

You may consider if further interventions are needed in these areas:

- Counseling
- Screening or referral
- Instructional support
- Parent conference

Counselor: Complete and retain a copy of ISS Student Information along with this sheet before routing this to the student's teacher(s).

Date routed: _____   Routed to: _____ ‖ Date routed: _____   Routed to: _____

_____   _____ ‖ _____   _____

_____   _____ ‖ _____   _____

_____   _____ ‖ _____   _____

_____ ‖ _____

Attached: Copy of ISS Student Information Sheet

SECTION 2: CORRECTIVE ACTION

Directions:

1) Print your first and last name and date on the spaces provided.

_____

      Student's Name   **Date**

2) Read the information below.

Your principal can take steps to help you know that your behavior is not acceptable in school. Here are some of these steps your principal may be able to choose. The items marked with arrowheads show how that step may effect you.

Step 1: If you are assigned to In-School Suspension:
- You are not with your friends.
- You are missing your teachers' instructions.
- You are getting behind.
- You may have to be quiet all day.

Step 2: If your principal assigns out of school suspension:
- You are sent home.
- Your friends are in school.
- You are missing your work and getting behind.

Step 3: Some schools have a behavior intervention program. You might be assigned to this program.
- This program may or may not be housed in your school.
- The rules in this program are much stricter than they are at your school.
- Your friends will not be there.
- You are not getting the instruction from your regular teacher.

Step 4: Expulsion
- The school board, a group of adults, listens to what your principal has to say about how you misbehave in school.
- Sometimes they appoint a hearing officer to hear what your principal has to say about how you act in school.
- If you are expelled, you won't come back to school.
- Your friends will be going to the next grade, you won't. You have to repeat your grade.

SECTION 1:
WHY AM I HERE?

Directions:

1) Print your first and last name and date on the spaces provided.

_____

                    Student's Name   **Date**

2) Read the information below.

Your principal assigned you to In-School Suspension. Students are assigned to this program because of misbehavior in the classrooms, halls, on the bus or at school events.

Read these interventions your teachers, counselor or principals may have already made to try to help you manage your behavior.

Warnings

Your teacher may have already warned you about your behavior.

Lunch Detention

You may have already missed your regular lunch with your friends due to your behavior.

After-School Detention

You may have had to stay after school.

Calls or Conferences With Your Parents

Your teacher, counselor and/or principal may have contacted your parents by phone or had a conference with them.

Student Conference

Your teacher may have already talked to you.

Counselor

Your counselor may have already met with you and/or your parents to try to arrange a program to help you.

School Resource Officer

As a courtesy, your principal may have had your school resource officer speak to you.

ISS STUDENT INFORMATION SHEET

Directions:
1) Print your first and last name and date on the spaces provided.

_____

Student's Name   **Date**

2) Mark any item that might be causing you a problem or caused you to act up.
   Note: Your counselor will receive a copy of this sheet and may share it with your teachers to help you.

HOME AND FAMILY
❑ I have problems at home with my brothers or sisters.
❑ I have problems at home with the person who takes care of me.
❑ I have problems studying at home.
❑ I have problems with my mom's boyfriend.
❑ I have problems with my father's girlfriend.
❑ I have problems with my dad.
❑ I have problems with my mom.
❑ Other: _____
   _____
   _____

SCHOOL / CLASSROOM
❑ I have trouble reading.
❑ I don't understand what I read.
❑ I have trouble with math.
❑ I have trouble remembering what I learn.
❑ I am being bullied.
❑ I can't concentrate.
❑ I cheat sometimes.
❑ Other: _____
   _____
   _____

PHYSICAL / ENVIRONMENTAL CONCERNS
❑ I have trouble hearing.
❑ I have trouble seeing.
❑ I have trouble with my speech.
❑ I daydream a lot.
❑ I can't sit still.
❑ I have trouble paying attention.
❑ I get angry or mad at school.
❑ The lights bother me.
❑ I have trouble breathing.
❑ I feel sad.
❑ I feel like crying.
❑ I am trying to fit in.
❑ I need a friend.
❑ I am trying to be cool.
❑ Other students are mad at me.
❑ Other students bother me.
❑ Other: _____
   _____
   _____

ISS TEACHER CONTACT SHEET

ISS Proctor: Complete this sheet by filling in the student's name and date of assignment to ISS. Place a check mark by the lesson(s) the student completed today. Attach this to the ISS Student Information Sheet and route both to the counselor.

Student's Name   **Date**

This student was assigned to In-School Suspension on the date given. The principal assigned the lessons marked below along with Assignment: In-School Suspension and Decision-Making.

✔ Assignment – In-School Suspension

✔ Decision-Making

❑ Bullying   ❑ Conflicts and Resolution

❑ Bus Infraction   ❑ Organization and Study Skills

❑ Classroom and School Disruptions

These lessons provided the student with the following:

• Opportunity to give information about concerns he/she may have.

• Disciplinary steps an administrator might take.

• Information specific to his/her behavior

• Activities relevant to the behavior

• Steps to Improve

• Contract was available if administratively requested.

You may consider if further interventions are needed in these areas:

• Conference with your administrator or counselor

• Screening or referral

• Instructional support

• Parent conference

Counselor: Complete and retain a copy of ISS Student Information along with this sheet before routing this to the student's teacher(s).

Date routed: Routed to: Date routed: Routed to:

_____   _____   _____   _____

_____   _____   _____   _____

_____   _____   _____   _____

_____   _____   _____   _____

_____   _____   _____   _____

Attached: Copy of ISS Student Information Sheet

SECTION 2:
CORRECTIVE ACTION

Directions:
1) Print your first and last name and date on the spaces provided.

_____

Student's Name   **Date**

2) Read the Corrective Actions that your principal can take.

Corrective Action Possibilities: Since your behavior continues to bother others and/or disrupt other students' learning as well as your education, your principal has assigned you to In-School Suspension. This is a more serious step. These are steps, as they might normally progress, if you do not improve your behavior. The arrowheads show how these steps or interventions might effect you.

Step 1: In-School Suspension—When you are in In-School Suspension:
- You aren't with your friends.
- You are missing your teachers' instructions.
- You are getting behind.

Step 2: Out of School Suspension—When you are in out of school suspension:
- You are sent home.
- Your friends are still in school.
- You are missing your teachers' instructions.
- You are getting behind.

Step 3: Alternative behavior program—Your school may have a program at another school that your principal might send you to.
- You won't be coming to this school while you are there.
- You won't be in your regularly scheduled classes.
- Your friends will not be there.
- You may have to travel on a bus to a different school.
- The rules may be stricter at this school or program than at your regular school.

Step 4: Hearing officer/Tribunal—Your principal may take you before a hearing. At this hearing probation may be assigned.
- Probation lists terms under which you are allowed to remain in school.

Step 5: Expulsion: A school board decides whether to expel you or let you remain in school.
- You have to repeat your grade.
- Your friends will progress to the next grade level, you will not.

LESSON 2
DECISION-MAKING

Grades 4-6

Title	Suggested Time
Section 1 7 Steps to Good Decision-Making	5 minutes
Lunch Menu	5 minutes
Matching Decisions with Consequences	5 minutes
Good and Bad Decisions	10 minutes
Section 2 Keeper Sheet—Steps to Improve	5 minutes
Apply What You've Learned	30 minutes
TOTAL TIME	**1 hour**

Grades 7-9

Title	Suggested Time
Section 1 7 Steps to Good Decision-Making	5 minutes
Choices/Decisions/Consequences	5 minutes
Situations	5 minutes
Good and Bad Decisions	10 minutes
Section 2 Keeper Sheet—Steps to Improve	5 minutes
Apply What You've Learned	30 minutes
TOTAL TIME	**1 hour**

Grades 10-12

Title	Suggested Time
Section 1 7 Steps to Good Decision-Making	5 minutes
Decisions and Consequences	10 minutes
The Big Dance	15 minutes
Cool Group	15 minutes
Section 2 Keeper Sheet—Steps to Improve	5 minutes
Apply What You've Learned	30 minutes
TOTAL TIME	**1 hour**

SECTION 1:
7 STEPS TO GOOD DECISION-MAKING

Directions:

1) Print your first and last name and date on the spaces provided.

_____

Student's Name   **Date**

2) Read the information below.

Every decision that you make comes from the choices that you make.

Every decision has consequences.

Consequences are the things that happen after we make a decision.

7 STEPS TO GOOD DECISION-MAKING

Step 1: Situation—What is the situation?

Think about going to the lunchroom today. The situation is that you will have choices to make about what you want for lunch.

Step 2: Choice—What are your choices?

You look over what is offered for lunch. You may have to decide between pizza and a hamburger.

Step 3: Consider the consequences—Think before acting!

• If you eat what you like, then you are satisfied.
• If you don't like what you choose, then you might be hungry.
• If you pick the wrong item, then you may not like it.

Step 4: Gather Information—

Your friend might tell you the hamburger is better than pizza.
You may want the pizza. It is your choice.

Step 5: Time to decide—Make your decision.

You make a decision about what you want for lunch that day. You decide on pizza.

Step 6: Consequences—You either liked or did not like what you got for lunch.

Step 7: Take a look back—This is called reflecting.

Reflecting means to take time to think about if you made the right decision.
Next time you may pick another item.

ACTIVITY:
LUNCH MENU

Directions:
1) Print your first and last name and date on the spaces provided.

_____

          Student's Name   **Date**

2) Read this situation.

Situation: School Lunch
At school lunch, you have choices you can make. Look at this school lunch menu below and put a check mark by the choices you would make.

SCHOOL'S LUNCH MENU

Pick one:
- ❏ Hamburger with lettuce and tomato
- ❏ Hamburger pizza

Pick one:
- ❏ Chocolate Chip Cookie
- ❏ Peanut Butter Cookie

Pick one:
- ❏ Tossed salad with dressing
- ❏ Cherry Jell-O

Pick one:
- ❏ Chocolate milk
- ❏ Regular milk
- ❏ Strawberry-flavored milk

Choices: You looked at the different items and made a choice.

Decision: You picked what you wanted.

Consequences: The consequence is what happens after you make a decision. If you liked what you picked, then the result or consequence was a tasty lunch. If you did not like what you picked, then the result or consequence was that you did not like it.

Reflecting: Take a few minutes to think about whether you liked what you decided. If you did not like it, then you may decide to eat something different next time.

30

Grades 4-6
LESSON 2

reproducible
DECISION-MAKING

ACTIVITY: MATCHING DECISIONS AND CONSEQUENCES

Directions:
1) Print your first and last name and date on the spaces provided.

_____

Student's Name   **Date**

2) Read this information about decision-making.

Every decision that you make comes from the choices that you make.

Every decision has consequences.

Consequences are the things that happen after you make a decision.

GOOD CHOICES = GOOD DECISIONS = GOOD CONSEQUENCES
BAD CHOICES = BAD DECISIONS = BAD CONSEQUENCES

Directions:
1) Draw a line to connect good decisions with good consequences.
2) Draw a line to connect bad decisions with bad consequences.

Example:
Jane riding her bike with a helmet would match to *She rides the bike safely.*
This is a good decision with a good consequence.

Decision

Jane rides her bike with a helmet.

Lem does not turn in his homework.

J.D. gets an attitude with his dad.

Manfred eats all of his supper.

Lynn brings all her books home to study.

Consequences

He gets a zero for homework.

She rides the bicycle safely.

She gets all her studying done.

He is sent to his room.

He gets ice cream for dessert.

31

ACTIVITY:
GOOD AND BAD DECISIONS

Directions:

1) Print your first and last name and date on the spaces provided.

_____

Student's Name	**Date**

2) Read this information about decision-making.

> *Every decision that you make comes from the choices that you make.*
>
> *Every decision has consequences.*
>
> *Consequences are the things that happen after you make a decision.*

Directions:

Read the decision and then read its consequence. As you read each one, think about if it was a good decision or a bad decision.

DECISION	CONSEQUENCE
	This is what happened because of the decision each student made.
Chad eats 10 cookies before dinner.	Chad does not want dinner, his mom is mad.
Amy studies for her test each day.	Amy makes a B+, she is so happy.
Hosea tells his counselor he is being bullied.	Hosea's counselor gets the bully to stop bothering him.
Cassandra rides her bike without a helmet.	She fell, cut her eye and had to go to the nurse.
Bernard talks ugly to another student.	Bernard has to stand on the wall at lunch.
Elaine wants to talk to the new boy at lunch.	Elaine talks to the new boy at lunch.

ACTIVITY:
GOOD AND BAD DECISIONS, CONTINUED

Directions:
Look back over the decisions and consequences.

If the consequences were good, then the decision was good.
Write down the good decisions under the column labeled **Good Decision**.

If the consequences were bad, then the decision was bad.
Write down the bad decisions under the column labeled **Bad Decision**.

GOOD DECISION	BAD DECISION
example: Amy studies for her test each day.	*example: Chad eats 10 cookies before dinner.*

SECTION 2:
KEEPER SHEET—STEPS TO IMPROVE

Directions:

1) Print your first and last name and date on the spaces provided.

_____

Student's Name   **Date**

2) Keep this sheet to help you remember how to make a good decision.

7 STEPS TO GOOD DECISION-MAKING

Step 1: Situation—What is the situation?

It is lunchtime, there will be some items where you can make a choice.

Step 2: Choice—What are your choices or selections on the lunch line?

Step 3: Think before you act!

• If you eat what you like, then you are full.
• If you don't eat what you like, you get hungry.

Step 4: Gather Information—

If you talk to your friend in the lunch line, he/she might tell you the hamburger is better than school pizza. It is your decision.

Step 5: Time to decide—Make your decision.

Step 6: Consequences—You either liked or did not like what you picked for lunch.

Step 7: Take a look back—This is called reflecting.

Reflecting means to think about if you made the right decision.
Next time you are in the same situation, you may make a different decision or choice.

ACTIVITY:
APPLY WHAT YOU'VE LEARNED

Directions:

1) Print your first and last name and date on the spaces provided.

_____

           Student's Name   **Date**

2) Think about a decision you made recently.
    Answer the questions in the spaces provided.

1. What was the situation?

2. What decision did you make?

3. What were the consequences or what happened because of the decision you made?

4. Now that you've had this lesson, think about this situation again. List your choices?

5. Now, which one would you choose?

6. What do you think the consequences would be if you had made this decision?

SECTION 1:
7 STEPS TO GOOD DECISION-MAKING

Directions:
1) Print your first and last name and date on the spaces provided.

_____

     Student's Name   **Date**

2) Read the information below.

7 STEPS TO GOOD DECISION-MAKING

Step 1: Situation—What is the situation?

Think about your teacher's daily homework assignments.

Step 2: Choice—What are your choices in dealing with this situation?

Your choices might be:
- Taking your books and materials home and getting the homework done.
- Taking your books and materials home and choosing not to do your homework.

Step 3: Consider the consequences—Think before you act! Think about your choices.

- If you go home prepared and get it done, you may earn a better grade.
- If you choose not to do your homework, then your grade suffers and you are not as prepared.

Step 4: Gather Information—Gather suggestions from other people.

- Others may suggest you get your work done.
- Some of your friends may tell you not to do your homework.
- Your parent may urge you to do your homework.

Step 5: Time to decide—Make your decision.

You make your decision whether to do or not to do your homework.

Step 6: Consequences—The consequences are the result(s) of your decision.

- If you do your homework, you may get a better grade and show your teacher you are making an effort.
- If you don't do your homework, then your grade suffers and you are not as prepared.

Step 7: Reflecting is looking back over what you've done.

Reflecting means to take time to think about your decision. If you made a good decision, the consequences were good. If it was a bad decision, the consequences were not good.

ACTIVITY:
CHOICES/DECISIONS/CONSEQUENCES

Directions:

1) Print your first and last name and date on the spaces provided.

_____

Student's Name   **Date**

2) Read each situation and the choices given. Put a check mark by the best decision.

DECISIONS

1. A book report is due in three weeks, which is the best decision?
   - ❏ You read the book and write the report 3 days before it is due.
   - ❏ You read the book, but you don't write the report.
   - ❏ You read the book, write the report, and forget to proofread it.
   - ❏ You read the book, write the report, and lose it.

2. You like someone more than just a friend. Which is the best way to let them know your feelings?
   - ❏ You throw a pencil at this person to show you are interested.
   - ❏ You give this person a note.
   - ❏ You go to the person and tell him/her yourself about your feelings.
   - ❏ You ask your best friend to go and tell him/her that you are interested.

Directions:

Read each of the consequences below. Based on the decision you made above, put a check mark by the consequence you feel is the best.

CONSEQUENCES

1.
   - ❏ You read the book, wrote the report 3 days before it is due, and earned a 90.
   - ❏ You read the book and didn't write the report and made a zero.
   - ❏ You read the book, wrote the report, forgot to proofread it and made a 72.
   - ❏ You read the book, wrote the report, lost it, and earned a zero.

2.
   - ❏ You threw a pencil at the person you liked and got in trouble with the teacher.
   - ❏ You gave the person you liked a note and another student grabbed it.
   - ❏ You talked to the person about how you felt. The person likes you too.
   - ❏ You asked your best friend to go and tell the person you liked them. Your best friend forgets to deliver the message.

ACTIVITY: SITUATIONS

Directions:

1) Print your first and last name and date on the spaces provided.

_____

Student's Name   **Date**

2) Read each situation and the choices.
- Place a circle around the best possible decision you could make.
- Mark an "X" through the choices that you think are the wrong choices.
- Then on the line provided, write what you think the consequences will be for the best decision that you circled.

1. James is mad at this teacher for the D he earned on the history essay.

   • He stormed out of class.   • He read the comments on the paper.

   • He asked the teacher if he could redo it.   • He balled the paper up and tossed it in the trash.

   Consequence: _____

   _____

2. Juanita is upset with Dorinda for sitting by her boyfriend at lunch.

   • She gets in Dorinda's face and tells her to back off. • She ignored Dorinda.

   • She went to the counselor to discuss the situation.   • She shoved Dorinda into her locker.

   Consequence: _____

   _____

3. Rodriguez and Shen want to ask two girls to the dance.

   • Each boy called the girl he   • They asked the girls during lunch
     wanted to ask.   break in front of their friends.

   • They sent the girls notes.   • Rodriguez called the girl that Shen wanted to ask.

   Consequence: _____

   _____

ACTIVITY:
GOOD AND BAD DECISIONS

Directions:
1) Print your first and last name and date on the spaces provided.

_____

       Student's Name   **Date**

2) Read each situation. Look at the choices in each situation.
- Write *G* by the choice that led to the best decision with good consequences.
- Write *B* by the choices that led to bad decisions with bad consequences.

Example: Dave has a book report due in two weeks.

   G a. Dave chooses to begin to read his book when it is assigned. The consequence is that he earns a 92.

   B b. Dave chooses to wait until the night before the assignment is due and begins to read a 190-page book. The consequences are that he doesn't get it finished and makes a zero.

1. Cynthia is trying to decide whether to watch her favorite TV program or do her homework before basketball practice.

     _____a. Choice one is to watch TV first. Consequences are that she gets her homework done late and is tired the next day.

     _____b. Choice two is to do her homework before watching TV. Consequences are that she goes to ball practice and watches TV before going to bed.

     _____c. Choice three is to not do any homework. The consequence is that she earns a zero for a homework grade.

2. Walter is the class clown. His teacher is reviewing for a test. Walter has a 75 average.

     _____a. Walter chooses to focus on the teacher. Consequences are that he better understands the work and makes a better grade.

     _____b. Walter selects to joke and tease others during class. Consequences are that he does not hear what the teacher is says. He earns a grade of 72.

     _____c. Walter chooses to write a joke during the review. The consequence is that the teacher picked up the joke and gave him lunch detention.

SECTION 2:
KEEPER SHEET—STEPS TO IMPROVE

Directions:

1) Print your first and last name and date on the spaces provided.

_____

Student's Name   **Date**

2) Read over the information. Keep this sheet to help you remember how to make good decisions.

7 STEPS TO GOOD DECISION-MAKING

Step 1: Situation—What is the situation? What is going on?

Step 2: Choice—What are your choices that you have to think about before you make a decision?

Step 3: Consider the consequences—Think before you act! Think about each choice that you have before you. Think about what might happen as a result of each choice.

Step 4: Gather Information—Talk to friends, parents, teachers, counselors or administrators before you make a decision.

Step 5: Time to decide—You make your decision.

Step 6: Consequences—Consequences are what happen as a result of the decision you made.

Step 7: Reflecting—Reflecting is taking time to think or reflect about whether you liked what happened as a result of the decision you made. If you did not like the consequences, then you might make a better decision next time.

ACTIVITY:
APPLY WHAT YOU'VE LEARNED

Directions:

1) Print your first and last name and date on the spaces provided.

_____

      Student's Name   **Date**

2) Think about a decision you have made. Complete each item below. Use the back of this sheet if needed.

1. What was the situation?

2. What decision did you make?

3. What were the consequences or what happened because of the decision you made?

4. Now that you've had this lesson, think about this situation again. List your choices?

5. Now, which one would you choose?

6. What do you think the consequences would be if you had made this decision?

SECTION 1:
7 STEPS TO GOOD DECISION-MAKING

Directions:

1) Print your first and last name and date on the spaces provided.

_____

        Student's Name   **Date**

2) Read this information.

Information to make the right decision comes from a lot of people as you get older and prepare to complete high school, go to work or to college. Decisions may become life-altering. This makes good decision-making extremely important.

• Your parents have raised you to do what is right according to how they were raised.

• Your teachers may also have shared with you what is right and wrong to do at school.

• School rules are given to you so you know what you can and cannot do.

• Your friends give you advice.

Every decision comes from choices you make.
From the choices you make, you then make a decision.
Every decision has consequences for you.
Consequences are the results of your choices.

GOOD CHOICES = GOOD DECISIONS = GOOD CONSEQUENCES
BAD CHOICES = BAD DECISIONS = BAD CONSEQUENCES

7 STEPS TO GOOD DECISION MAKING

Step 1: Situation—What is the situation?

Step 2: Choice—What choices do you have?

Step 3: Consider the consequences—Think about each choice and what might happen as a result of each choice.

Step 4: Gather Information—Talk to friends, parents, teachers, counselors or administrators before you make a decision.

Step 5: Time to decide—Make your decision.

Step 6: Consequences—What happened as a result of the decision you made?

Step 7: Reflecting—Reflecting is taking time to think about whether you made the right decision. If you do this, and this type of situation comes up again, this may help you make a better decision next time.

ACTIVITY:
DECISIONS AND CONSEQUENCES

Directions:

1) Print your first and last name and date on the spaces provided.

_____

       Student's Name   **Date**

2) Read the information below.

- Place a D by the decision and a C by the consequence.

- In the 3rd blank, write a GC if this was a good consequence. Write a BC if this was a bad consequence.

Example:

1. __D__ Jennifer decides to ask Ben to the dance, he tells her "No". She hits him.

   __C__ A teacher sees her and she does not get to come to the dance. .... __BC__

2. _____ Ramona tells her teacher to "Shut up!" when he calls her down for talking in class.

   _____ The teacher writes her up for disrespect. .... _____

3. _____ Harold decides to hit Amanda's rear end while walking behind her in the hall.

   _____ The school resource officer sees him and charges him. .... _____

4. _____ Rodriguez sees Agatha cheating on a test.

   _____ He reports this to his teacher. Agatha earns a zero. .... _____

5. _____ Susan wants to attend a local technical college.
             She is late turning in her application.

   _____ The technical college writes her a letter rejecting
             her application because it is late. .... _____

6. _____ The Scholastic Aptitude Test is scheduled for December.
             Henry gets his application in on time.

   _____ He receives his ticket for admission and takes the test. .... _____

ACTIVITY:
THE BIG DANCE

Directions:

1) Print your first and last name and date on the spaces provided.

_____

Student's Name   **Date**

2) Read the story.

THE BIG DANCE

Jennifer and James have been friends since the ninth grade. James is on the chess team and Jennifer is a volleyball player. Their interests are different, but lately James has been hanging around Jennifer's locker after school.

James has a best friend, Adam. Adam is also on the chess team and he and James are best friends. Adam does not like Jennifer. Jennifer's best friend has secretly told Adam that she likes James. The homecoming dance is coming up and James wants to ask Jennifer to go. James is not sure how to ask her.

---

3) Now that you've read the story, turn to the next page and answer the questions based on the story and what you've learned.

ACTIVITY:
THE BIG DANCE, CONTINUED

Directions:

1) Print your first and last name and date on the spaces provided.

_____

Student's Name   **Date**

2) Read each question and place a check mark(s) in the space(s) that you feel best answers the question.

1. What is the situation?

   ❏ Adam wants to take Jennifer to the dance.

   ❏ Jennifer does not like James.

   ❏ James wants to ask Jennifer to the dance.

2. Of the choices listed, which one do you feel is the best choice for James?

   ❏ James could ask Adam to ask Jennifer for him.

   ❏ James could ask Jennifer's friends what she thinks.

   ❏ James could ask Jennifer while they walk together to the canteen.

   ❏ James could just be friends with Adam and forget about Jennifer.

3. If James wanted to gather some information to help him, place a check
   mark by the people with whom he might talk. Pick more than one.

   ❏ Parents   ❏ Adam   ❏ Counselor

   ❏ Teacher   ❏ Other friends ❏ Jennifer's best friend who likes him as well.

4. James is ready to make a decision. Which decision will he make?

   ❏ James will ask another girl to the dance.

   ❏ James will ask Jennifer to the dance.

   ❏ James will hang out with Adam and forget about the dance.

   ❏ James will not go to the dance.

ACTIVITY:
COOL GROUP

Directions:
1) Print your first and last name and date on the spaces provided.

_____

      Student's Name   **Date**

2) Read this situation.

COOL GROUP

Francesca Yanez and Danielle are best friends. Lately, Danielle is upset because Francesca has been ignoring her. Francesca wants to be a part of the cool group at school, Danielle does not want to be a part of this group of girls. The cool girls keep ignoring Francesca. Reynaldo tells Francesca that they smoke in the bathroom, sneak out at night and smoke marijuana.

---

3) Read these choices that Francesca can make. Under each choice, write down what you think the consequence will be for each of the choices she could make.

Choice 1:   Francesca should keep trying to talk to the girls in this cool group.

Consequence: _____

_____

Choice 2:   Francesca needs to talk to Danielle and see why she is upset.

Consequence: _____

_____

Choice 3:   Francesca ought to talk to her parents or school counselor about what she wants.

Consequence: _____

_____

Choice 4:   Francesca needs to listen to Reynaldo and return to her friend, Danielle.

Consequence: _____

_____

SECTION 2:
KEEPER SHEET—STEPS TO IMPROVE

Directions:

1) Print your first and last name and date on the spaces provided.

_____

Student's Name   **Date**

2) Read over the information. Keep this sheet to help you remember how to make good decisions.

7 STEPS TO GOOD DECISION-MAKING

Step 1: Situation—What is the situation?

Step 2: Choice—What are your choices in dealing with this situation?

Step 3: Consider the consequences—Think before you act! What might the results of your choices?

Step 4: Gather Information—Talk to parents, teachers, counselors, and friends to help you look at the possibilities.

Step 5: Time to decide—Make your decision.

Step 6: Consequences—Consequences are the results of your decision.

Step 7: Reflecting—Reflecting means to take time to think about whether or not you made the right decision.

ACTIVITY:
APPLY WHAT YOU'VE LEARNED

Directions:

1) Print your first and last name and date on the spaces provided.

_____

| **Student's Name** | **Date** |

2) Write about a decision you made recently. Use the back of this sheet if needed.
   Be sure to include the following:

    1. Explain the situation.

    2. List the choices you had.

    3. Tell what your decision was.

    4. What were the consequences?

    5. If you gathered information, explain this.

    6. If you had this decision to make again, explain what you might do differently.

LESSON 3
BULLYING

Grades 4-6

Title	Suggested Time
Section 1 Bully, Victim, and Bystander	5 minutes
Section 2 Types of Bullying	5 minutes
Lunch Crisis	10 minutes
Matching	10 minutes
Eddie's Bullies	10 minutes
Section 3 Keeper Sheet – Steps to Improve	5 minutes
Apply What You've Learned	30 minutes
Section 4 Contract	5 minutes
TOTAL TIME	**1 hour 20 minutes**

Grades 7-9

Title	Suggested Time
Section 1 Bully, Victim and Bystander	5 minutes
Section 2 Types of Bullying	5 minutes
Twins	10 minutes
Ray's Fears	10 minutes
Identifying Roles	10 minutes
Section 3 Keeper Sheet – Steps to Improve	5 minutes
Apply What You've Learned	30 minutes
Section 4 Contract	5 minutes
TOTAL TIME	**1 hour 20 minutes**

Grades 10-12

Title	Suggested Time
Section 1 Bully, Victim and Bystander	5 minutes
Section 2 Types of Bullying	5 minutes
Jason Erupts	10 minutes
Identify Roles	10 minutes
Identify Types of Bullying	10 minutes
Section 3 Keeper Sheet – Steps to Improve	5 minutes
Apply What You've Learned	30 minutes
Section 4 Contract	5 minutes
TOTAL TIME	**1 hour 20 minutes**

SECTION 1:
BULLY, VICTIM, AND BYSTANDER

Directions:

1) Print your first and last name and date on the spaces provided.

_____

       Student's Name   **Date**

2) Read the information below.

BULLIES...

are people who make a habit of hurting younger, weaker or smaller people.

They hurt others by what they say or by what they do.

VICTIMS...

are the people who are hurt by what the bully says or does.

Victims usually have not done anything to bother or hurt the bully.

Victims don't feel very good about themselves and sometimes

they don't want to come to school or go to class.

BYSTANDERS...

are the people who watch the bully hurting the victim.

Some bystanders take the side of the bully.

Some stand by and do nothing. Sometimes, a bystander

will show great character and reach out to help the victim.

SECTION 2:
TYPES OF BULLYING

Directions:

1) Print your first and last name and date on the spaces provided.

_____

        Student's Name   **Date**

2) Read the information below.

TYPES OF BULLYING:

Chat rooms
When you use computer chat rooms to write words that hurt others, this is a form of bullying.

Email
When you use email to write untruthful things or hurtful things, this is bullying.

Gossip
Gossip is a form of bullying. Gossip is when you tell things that you have heard about other people.

Hitting, pushing, and shoving other students is how some students bully others.

Inappropriate talk, touch or gestures
When you say something hurtful, this is bullying. If you touch
someone or use your body to hurt someone, this is bullying.

Name-calling
When you call someone a hurtful name.

Note passing
Writing hurtful words about other students is bullying.

Rumors
Telling others untruthful and hurtful things about others is bullying.

Spitting
When you spit on another student on purpose, this is bullying.

Telephone calls
Using the telephone to talk about others in a hurtful or untruthful way is bullying.

ACTIVITY:
LUNCH CRISIS

Directions:

1) Print your first and last name and date on the spaces provided.

_____

        Student's Name   **Date**

2) Read the information below and answer the questions.

LUNCH CRISIS

Everyday at lunch, Thomas tells Stephen that he cannot sit down unless he brings him a treat for lunch. Stephen is afraid of Thomas. Stephen tells his mom that he has got to have an extra treat for lunch the next day. His mom thinks this is odd. The next day, Stephen tells him mom he needs another treat. His mom is worried and asks him why he has to bring extra food. Stephen tells his mom that Thomas won't leave him alone Even when he brings the extra treat, Thomas still won't let him sit down at lunch.

---

1. Who is the bully?

   _____

2. What is Thomas doing to bully Stephen?

   _____

   _____

3. Why do you think Stephen didn't tell his mom about Thomas the first time?

   _____

   _____

4. Do you think Stephen did the right thing by telling his mom? Explain why you answered yes or no.

   _____

   _____

5. What should Stephen's mom do?

   _____

   _____

ACTIVITY: MATCHING

Directions:
1) Print your first and last name and date on the spaces provided.

_____

       Student's Name   **Date**

2) Read each situation. Draw a line from the situation to the name of the bully. The information in parenthesis shows you what type of bullying this is.

Example:

In the first situation, Myra is the bully. Draw a line from that situation to Myra's name on the right side of the page.

Situation	The Bully
Myra shoves Ternisha in the hall (Hitting, shoving or pushing)	Lyn
D. J. tells Samantha that she is a slob. (Name-calling)	Cindy
Bernard is getting shoved by Ben.	Bob
Cindy told everybody in gym class that Renee has lice. (Spreading rumors)	Melissa
Melissa pinched Josh on his bottom. (Inappropriate touch)	Ben
Amos is getting calls from Bob. Bob is spreading rumors about Jessica (Telephone)	Myra
Lyn passes Melinda a note about Jessica. (Note passing)	D. J.

ACTIVITY:
EDDIE'S BULLIES

Directions:

1) Print your first and last name and date on the spaces provided.

_____

Student's Name   **Date**

2) Read the story. Then read each situation. Put a circle around either True or False, whichever is correct.

EDDIE'S BULLIES

Eddie is a 6th grader. He has been bullied a long time. At lunch, Nathan grabbed his book bag and threw his note cards across the grass. Then Nathan took Eddie's drink. He opened it and threw it.

Eddie got mad and went to his guidance counselor. Eddie did not want to meet with Nathan. When the counselor talked to Nathan, he told her that Eddie needed to toughen up. The counselor told Nathan that he was to stop bothering Eddie immediately and leave him alone. Since this was the 2nd time that Nathan had bullied Eddie, the counselor sent him to the principal.

1. Eddie has been bullied for several years. ....True   False

2. Nathan grabbed his book bag. ....True   False

3. Nathan drank Eddie's drink...True   False

4. Eddie is the bully. ....True   False

5. Nathan is the bully. ....True   False

6. Nathan has bothered Eddie before. ....True   False

7. Eddie did the right thing to report this to his counselor. ....True   False

8. The counselor did the right thing to report this incident to the principal. ....True   False

SECTION 3:
KEEPER SHEET—STEPS TO IMPROVE

Directions:
1) Print your first and last name and date on the spaces provided.

_____

Student's Name   **Date**

2) Read the information below. Keep this sheet to remind you of ways to keep from bullying others.

STEPS TO IMPROVE

- *Learn to respect others.*

- *Talk to your counselor or teachers when you are upset.*

- *Tell your counselor or teacher when you feel like you are going to bully another student.*

- *Tell you counselor if you are being bullied at home by a brother, sister or parent.*

- *Everybody is not like you. You may not like what other people do. This is not a reason to bully them.*

- *Tell your friends that you will not join in a bullying situation.*

- *Talk with your parents, teachers or counselors if you are not sure how to handle a situation.*

ACTIVITY:
APPLY WHAT YOU'VE LEARNED

Directions:
1) Print your first and last name and date on the spaces provided.

_____

      Student's Name   **Date**

2) Answers the questions below.

  1. Who did you bully?

    _____

  2. Why did you bully this student and what did you do to bully this student?

    _____

    _____

    _____

    _____

  3. Had this student done anything to hurt or bother you?

    _____

    _____

  4. Look over the Steps to Improve. List at least 3 steps you will take to improve.
    1. _____
    2. _____
    3. _____

  5. What did you learn from the lesson today? Use the back of this sheet to write down this answer if needed.

    _____

    _____

    _____

SECTION 4:
CONTRACT

Directions:
1) Print your first and last name and date on the spaces provided.

_____

       Student's Name   **Date**

2) Read this contract carefully. Put a check mark by the items you are willing to work on.
   By signing this contract, you are saying that you will do these things to improve your behavior.

CONTRACT

❑ **I will stop bullying other students at this school.**

❑ **If I feel like I'm going to hurt another student, I will talk to my counselor or other adult at this school before I bully.**

❑ **I will report myself if I say anything or do anything hurtful to another student.**

❑ **I will see my counselor to learn to respect myself.**

❑ **I will make a report to my counselor if I feel I am being bullied at home.**

**I know that if my behavior does not get better that the
principal may take further action. I know that the work
I've done today will be placed in my folder. It will show
that the school has tried to help me improve or get better.**

Sign your name in cursive writing: _____

SECTION 1:
BULLY, VICTIM AND BYSTANDER

Directions:
1) Print your first and last name and date on the spaces provided.

_____

       Student's Name   **Date**

2) Read the information below about bullies, victims and bystanders:

BULLIES...

are people who make a habit of hurting younger, weaker or smaller people.

They hurt others by what they say or by what they do.

VICTIMS...

are the people who suffer from what the bully says or does.

Victims usually have not done anything to bother or hurt the bully.

Victims sometimes think about killing themselves.

They don't feel good about themselves,

and sometimes do not want to come to school.

BYSTANDERS...

are the people who watch the bully hurting the victim.

Some bystanders take the side of the bully.

Some bystanders stand by and do nothing. Sometimes, a bystander

will show great character and reach out to help the victim.

SECTION 2:
TYPES OF BULLYING

Directions:
1) Print your first and last name and date on the spaces provided.

Student's Name | **Date**

2) Read the information below.

TYPES OF BULLYING:

Chat rooms
When you use computer chat rooms to write rumors, put downs
or say hurtful things about other people, this is bullying.

Email
Bullying is using email to spread gossip, write
rumors, use racial slurs or put down other people.

Gossip
Telling things you have heard about others is a form of bullying.

Hitting, pushing, and shoving other students is a way to bully others.

Inappropriate talk/gestures
Making unwanted comments or using any part of your
body to send an unwanted message is bullying.

Inappropriate touch
Bullying also occurs when you touch someone's body and they do not want you to.

Name-calling
Calling people racial slurs or names that have sexual meanings is also bullying.

Note passing
Writing untruthful or hurtful things about other students is another form of bullying.

Rumors
Telling untruthful and hurtful things about someone is bullying.

Spitting
When you decide to spit on someone, this is bullying.

Telephone calls
Using the telephone to talk about others in a hurtful or untruthful way is bullying.

ACTIVITY:
TWINS

Directions:

1) Print your first and last name and date on the spaces provided.

_____

Student's Name   **Date**

2) Read the information below.

TWINS

Danielle and Jessica are new friends. They wear the same thing everyday and fix their hair the same everyday. Charles and Leonard see that Danielle and Jessica are looking good. However, they have also noticed that Danielle and Jessica are picking on Emma. Charles saw Jessica roll her eyes at Emma. Leonard saw Danielle push Emma into her locker. Both boys know that Emma is getting frustrated and is missing school. However, both boys are still considering taking Danielle and Jessica to the first basketball game. Yet, they do not like what they see these girls do to Emma.

Charles decides to talk to Danielle and Jessica. He tells them that Emma is a friend and that he and Leonard like them, but they want the bullying to stop. Jessica tells him that Emma is just a little "wart" and that they are going to get her after the basketball game.

ACTIVITY:
TWINS, CONTINUED

Directions:
1) Print your first and last name and date on the spaces provided.

_____

        Student's Name   **Date**

2) Answer these questions:

List the names of the bullies in this story. _____

Who are the bystanders? _____

Who is the victim? _____

List the ways that Danielle and Jessica are bullying or are planning to bully Emma.

_____

_____

_____

_____

How does being bullied make Emma feel?

_____

_____

_____

What did Charles tell Danielle and Jessica about bullying Emma?

_____

_____

What was Jessica's response to Charles when he talked to her about her bullying Emma?

_____

_____

What do you think Charles needs to do with the information about Jessica and Danielle "getting" Emma after the game?

_____

_____

_____

ACTIVITY:
RAY'S FEARS

Directions:
1) Print your first and last name and date on the spaces provided.

_____

Student's Name   **Date**

2) Read the story below.

RAY'S FEARS

Ray is afraid during P.E. class. Ray tells Ben, his best friend, that Sid and Ramos bully him by punching him in the stomach and calling him names. When Ray goes into the gym, Sid comes up and pulls his gym shorts down around his thighs. Sid then takes a towel and pops Ray.

Ray tells Ben that he is sick and does not want to go to Physical Education. The next day Ray is not in school. Ben is worried about him. Ben is also afraid of Sid and Ramos as he has seen them in action.

Ben goes to his coach and tells him of the situation with Ray, Sid and Ramos. The coach tells Ben to tell Ray to ignore Sid and Ramos and that they won't bother him any more. Sid and Ramos keep bullying him. At this point, Ben decides he will go to the counselor. The counselor turns the complaint into the principal. Sid and Ramos are suspended from school for bullying Ray. The parents of Sid and Ramos are required to come in for a parent conference. The principal put both boys on probation as this was the second report of bullying.

The terms of probation include the following:
- Sid and Ramos are not allowed in the halls until the halls are clear.

- Sid and Ramos are removed from Physical Education for the rest of the year.

ACTIVITY:
RAY'S FEARS, CONTINUED

Directions:

1) Print your first and last name and date on the spaces provided.

_____

Student's Name   **Date**

2) Circle True or False to correctly answer the situation described.

True   *False*   The two bullies are Ray and Ben.

True   *False*   Ray is the current victim.

True   *False*   The bullies have pulled Ray's shorts down
                       and popped him with a towel.

True   *False*   Sid and Ramos are just teasing Ray; they are not bullying him.

True   *False*   Ben is a bystander who decided to help Ray.

True   *False*   The coach helped Ray.

True   *False*   Ignoring the situation worked.

True   *False*   Ben, the bystander, chose to tell the counselor.

True   *False*   The counselor just ignored Ben's complaint.

True   *False*   The principal expelled Sid and Ramos.

ACTIVITY:
IDENTIFYING ROLES

Directions:

1) Print your first and last name and date on the spaces provided.

_____

         Student's Name   **Date**

2) Read each situation below. Write down the name of the bully, the victim and the bystander. Use Section 2 of this lesson to list the type of bullying that was done by the bully.

Situation: Jane and Samuel like each other. However, Mandy sends him a note telling him lies about Jane. When Jane finds out what Mandy wrote, she is embarrassed and mad.

Bullies: _____

Victims: _____

Bystanders: _____

Types of Bullying: _____

Situation: Wyatt and D.J. have been pushing Leon and Randy in the halls. Nora, Lindsay and Hosea have been watching Leon and Randy get hurt. They are afraid and don't want to say anything to these students.

Bullies: _____

Victims: _____

Bystanders: _____

Types of Bullying: _____

Situation: Melissa, Melinda and Breanna recently enrolled in a new school. They see that Hannah's group is the coolest group of girls. They tried to sit with them at lunch and Hannah name-called them. Then Hannah started telling the other girls untrue stories about Melissa. Melissa started crying. Hannah told her she was a baby. Hannah got on the phone and told her friends that Melissa was a baby.

Bullies: _____

Victims: _____

Bystanders: _____

Types of Bullying: _____

Grades 7-9
LESSON 3

BULLYING

SECTION 3:
KEEPER SHEET—STEPS TO IMPROVE

Directions:

1) Print your first and last name and date on the spaces provided.

_____

Student's Name   **Date**

2) Read the information below. Keep this sheet to help you remember these steps.

STEPS TO IMPROVE

- *Learn to respect yourself. See your counselor to determine your strengths and weaknesses, learn about your interests, and match your interests with career fields.*

- *Talk to your counselor or teachers when you are upset about issues with other students.*

- *Tell your counselor or teacher when you feel the urge to bully another student or when you pick out someone to bully.*

- *Tell your counselor if you are being bullied at home.*

- *Realize that everyone is not like you. You may disagree with other people. This is not a reason to bully another.*

- *Tell other students that you will not join in a bullying situation.*

- *Talk with your parents, teachers or counselors if you are not sure how to handle a situation.*

ACTIVITY:
APPLY WHAT YOU'VE LEARNED

Directions:

1) Print your first and last name and date on the spaces provided.

_____

      Student's Name   **Date**

2) Write a paragraph that describes the situation that caused you to be assigned to In-School Suspension.

    1) Explain how you bullied your victim. Use Section 2 if needed.

    2) Explain why you bullied this student.

    3) List some steps you could take to improve your behavior.

Example:

I was assigned to In-School Suspension because I bullied Matilda Renos. I bullied her by spreading rumors. I told other people that she was a fat heifer. I don't like Matilda Renos. She wants to go out with my boyfriend. I guess I could have gone to my counselor and we could have talked about ways to let Matilda know how I was feeling.

_____

_____

_____

_____

_____

_____

_____

_____

SECTION 4:
CONTRACT

Directions:
1) Print your first and last name and date on the spaces provided.

_____

          Student's Name   **Date**

2) Read this contract carefully. Put a check mark by the items you are willing to work on.
   By signing this contract, you are making a commitment to take steps to improve your behavior.

CONTRACT

❑ **I will stop bullying other students at this school.**

❑ **If I feel the urge to bully another student, I will talk to
the counselor or other adult at this school before I bully.**

❑ **If I say anything or do anything hurtful to another student,
I will report this to my principal, teacher or counselor.**

❑ **I will see my counselor to learn to respect myself.**

❑ **I will be respectful to other students and adults at my school.**

❑ **I will work toward being a helpful bystander by reporting
incidents of bullying to an adult at school or my parent.**

**I understand that if I do not improve my behavior that
the principal may take further disciplinary action. I understand
that this packet will be placed in my file to show that the
school has presented me with information to help me improve.**

Sign your name: _____

SECTION 1:
BULLY, VICTIM AND BYSTANDER

Directions:

1) Print your first and last name and date on the spaces provided.

_____

    Student's Name   **Date**

2) Read the information below about bullies, victims and bystanders.

BULLIES...

are people who make a habit of hurting younger, weaker or smaller people.

They hurt others by what they say or by what they do.

Bullies like having power over another person.

VICTIMS...

are the people who suffer from what the bully says or does.

Victims usually have not done anything to bother or hurt the bully.

Sometimes victims think about killing themselves, don't feel

good about themselves, and do not want to come to school.

BYSTANDERS...

are the people who watch the bully hurting the victim.

Sometimes the bystanders take the side of the bully.

Sometimes they stand by and do nothing. Sometimes, a bystander

will show great character and reach out to help the victim.

SECTION 2:
TYPES OF BULLYING

Directions:

1) Print your first and last name and date on the spaces provided.

_____

          Student's Name   **Date**

2) Read the information below.

TYPES OF BULLYING:

Chat rooms
When you use a computer chat room to write rumors, put downs
or say hurtful things about other people, this is bullying.

Email
Bullying is using email to spread gossip, write
rumors, use racial slurs or put people down.

Gossip
Telling things you have heard about others is a form of bullying.

Hitting, pushing, and shoving other students is a way to bully others.

Inappropriate talk/gestures
Making unwanted comments or using any part of your body to send an unwanted message is bullying.

Inappropriate touch
Bullying also occurs when you touch someone's body and they do not want you to do this.

Name-calling
Calling people racial slurs or names that have sexual meanings is bullying.

Note passing
Writing untruthful or hurtful things about other students is another form of bullying.

Rumors
Telling untruthful and hurtful things about someone is bullying.

Spitting
When you decide to spit on someone, this is bullying.

Telephone calls
Using the telephone to talk about others in a hurtful or untruthful way is bullying.

ACTIVITY:
JASON ERUPTS

Directions:

1) Print your first and last name and date on the spaces provided.

_____   _____

Student's Name   **Date**

2) Read the story below.

JASON ERUPTS

"I'm really hot, I feel like I'm going to explode," Jason exclaimed. His counselor, Mrs. Jamison, throws Jason a stress-relieving ball. "Do you know they've been at this since third grade and now I'm in 10th? They are at it again. I've told them to stop, but they won't. Ben, Robbie and Amy told me that no one wants to be friends with me. Then Ben dashed by me, shoved me and took my book bag. He went into my wallet, took all my money and threw it into the parking lot. I've had all I can take. Sam was a witness, but he just stood there."

Last week when I tried to sit down in the lunchroom, Robbie said, 'Don't let that fatty sit here.' They don't own the lunchroom or the seats; I can sit wherever I want to sit. When I am in class, I can hear them whispering my name. Then I heard Amy giggle. On Monday, Amy threw a spitball and hit my head. I turned around and told her to stop. I heard Robbie call me gay. I'm not gay. I am as much of a man as Robbie and Ben are," Jason said.

ACTIVITY:
JASON ERUPTS, CONTINUED

Directions:
1) Print your first and last name and date on the spaces provided.

_____

         Student's Name   **Date**

2) Answer these questions from the story, **Jason Erupts**.

   1. Who are the bullies? _____

   2. What are the ways that Jason was bullied?

        _____

        _____

   3. Did the victim do anything to bring this upon himself?

        _____

        _____

   4. How do you think the victim feels when he is bullied?

        _____

        _____

   5. Were there any bystanders?

        _____

        _____

   6. What was the reaction of the bystanders?

        _____

        _____

   7. What did the victim do to get them to stop? Please explain.

        _____

        _____

   8. How do you think the bullies feel when they bully him?

        _____

        _____

ACTIVITY:
IDENTIFY ROLES

Directions:

1) Print your first and last name and date on the spaces provided.

_____

Student's Name   **Date**

2) Read each situation. Identify the bully(s), the victim(s) and the bystander(s). Write down how the bystanders reacted. Use Section 2 of this lesson to list the type(s) of bullying that was done by the bully.

Situation: Michael recently entered high school. Few people know this, but their home burned down and his family lost everything. Carolyn is from a wealthy family with plenty of money. When she sees Michael she laughs at him and calls him names and makes fun of this clothes. George and Susan hear her.

Bullies: _____

Victims: _____

Bystanders: _____

Reaction of Bystanders: _____

Types of Bullying: _____

_____

Situation: Jennifer and Brad are going together. Breanna really likes Brad and she decides she is going to get him away from Jennifer. Breanna writes Brad a note and tells him some untruthful things that Jennifer has done with his best friend, Chris. Jennifer's friend Linda learns about the note and tells Jennifer. Breanna gives the note to Brad.

Bullies: _____

Victims: _____

Bystanders: _____

Reaction of Bystanders: _____

_____

Types of Bullying: _____

_____

ACTIVITY:
IDENTIFY ROLES, CONTINUED

Directions:

1) Print your first and last name and date on the spaces provided.

_____

      Student's Name   ***Date***

2) Read each situation. Identify the bully(s), the victim(s) and the bystander(s). Write down how the bystanders reacted. Use Section 2 of this lesson to list the type(s) of bullying that was done by the bully.

Situation: Wesley is a member of the football team. He has been playing quarterback since 10th grade. When he joined the new high school team, he heard some of the high school players put him down. Recently, in the weight room, Harold came and shoved him into the lockers. Harold wants to play quarterback. Samuel saw this, but he did not do anything. Two days later, Harold called him, "gay".

Bullies: _____

Victims: _____

Bystanders: _____

Reaction of Bystanders: _____

Types of Bullying: _____

_____

Situation: Karen is on the Cross Country team. Recently Revonda has joined the team, having moved from a rival high school. They are now both of the same team. Their teamwork is critical for the performance of the team as a whole. During a recent race, Revonda purposefully tripped Karen in the last mile of the three-mile race. The incident caused Karen to sprain her ankle and she limped across the finish line.

Bullies: _____

Victims: _____

Bystanders: _____

Reaction of Bystanders: _____

Types of Bullying: _____

_____

ACTIVITY:
IDENTIFY TYPES OF BULLYING

Directions:
1) Print your first and last name and date on the spaces provided.

_____

Student's Name   **Date**

2) Read each situation. Place a circle around the types of bullying demonstrated in each situation.

1. Samuel wrote Josetta through a chat room and told her that Hilda was dating some dude at another high school. Hilda found out about this untruth and decided she would get Samuel back. Hilda called three of her friends and told them that Samuel was a liar and a jerk. When Samuel arrived at school, Hilda spit on him and shoved him into the brick steps at school. Samuel was furious so he called Hilda an inappropriate sexual name and threw his hand up in the air with an inappropriate gesture toward her.

Chat rooms	**Email**	**Gossip**
Hitting, pushing, shoving	**Inappropriate gestures**	**Note passing**
Inappropriate talk	**Inappropriate touch**	**Name calling**
Rumors	**Spitting**	**Telephone calls**

In the space below, explain how Hilda became the bully. Then explain how she could have handled this situation better.

_____

_____

_____

_____

_____

_____

_____

ACTIVITY:
IDENTIFY TYPES OF BULLYING, CONTINUED

2. In the hall, Louise said to Casey, "Um, um good." Then she ran her eyes up and down his body. Casey does not like Louise and considered the message offensive. Then Louise passed him a note telling him that he was hot. Casey did not respond. Then Louise told everyone that she was going with Casey. At this point, Casey had enough and told Louise to back off and that he was not interested in her. Louise did not back off and started to write him love notes.

Chat rooms	**Email**	**Gossip**
Hitting, pushing, shoving	**Inappropriate gestures**	**Note passing**
Inappropriate talk	**Inappropriate touch**	**Name calling**
Rumors	**Spitting**	**Telephone calls**

In the space below, explain how Casey was bullied. What do you think he needs to do now?

_____

_____

_____

_____

_____

_____

_____

SECTION 3:
KEEPER SHEET—STEPS TO IMPROVE

Directions:

1) Print your first and last name and date on the spaces provided.

_____

Student's Name   **Date**

2) Read the information below. Keep this sheet to help remind you how to improve.

STEPS TO IMPROVE

- *Learn to respect yourself. See your counselor to determine your strengths and weaknesses and ways you can learn more about your unique gifts. Your counselor can help look at your interests and help you learn about what jobs you might be interested in when you get out of school.*

- *Talk to your counselor or teachers when you are upset about issues with other students.*

- *Tell your counselor or teacher when you feel the urge to bully another student or when you have picked out your victim.*

- *Tell your counselor if you are being bullied at home.*

- *Realize that everyone is not like you. You may disagree with other people. This is not a reason to bully another.*

- *Tell other bullies that you will not join in a bullying situation.*

- *Talk with your parents, teachers or counselors if you are not sure how to handle a situation.*

ACTIVITY:
APPLY WHAT YOU'VE LEARNED

Directions:

1) Print your first and last name and date on the spaces provided.

_____

          Student's Name   **Date**

2) Write a paragraph that describes the situation that caused you to be assigned to In-School Suspension. Explain how and why you bullied the person. List three steps that you will take to improve.

_____

_____

_____

_____

_____

_____

_____

_____

_____

_____

_____

_____

_____

_____

SECTION 4:
CONTRACT

Directions:

1) Print your first and last name and date on the spaces provided.

_____

Student's Name   **Date**

2) Read this contract carefully. Then put a check mark by items you'll work on.
By signing this contract, you are making a commitment to improve your behavior.

CONTRACT

❑ **I will stop bullying other students at this school.**

❑ **If I feel the urge to bully another student, I will seek the assistance of my counselor or other adult at this school before I bully.**

❑ **If I say anything or do anything hurtful to another student or adult at this school, I will report this to my principal or counselor.**

❑ **I will see my counselor to learn to respect myself.**

❑ **I will be respectful to other students and adults at my school.**

❑ **I will work toward being a helpful bystander by reporting incidents of bullying to an adult at school or my parent.**

I understand that if I do not improve my behavior that the principal may take further disciplinary action. I understand that this packet will be placed in my file to show that the school has presented me with information to help me improve.

Student's Signature: _____

LESSON 4
BUS INFRACTIONS

Grades 4-6

Title	Suggested Time
Section 1 Misbehaving	5 minutes
Alisha's Hurt Feelings	10 minutes
Good and Bad Choices	10 minutes
The Group	10 minutes
Section 2 Keeper Sheet - Steps to Improve	5 minutes
Apply What You've Learned	30 minutes
Section 3 Contract	5 minutes
TOTAL TIME	**1 hour 15 minutes**

Grades 7-9

Title	Suggested Time
Section 1 What's a Bus Infraction?	5 minutes
Damion Shows Courage	10 minutes
Jozetta Acts Out	10 minutes
William's Problem	10 minutes
Section 2 Keeper Sheet - Steps to Improve	5 minutes
Apply What You've Learned	30 minutes
Section 3 Contract	5 minutes
TOTAL TIME	**1 hour 15 minutes**

Grades 10-12

Title	Suggested Time
Section 1 Definition – Bus Infraction	5 minutes
Theft	15 minutes
Drugs	15 minutes
Out of the Window	15 minutes
Section 2 Keeper Sheet - Steps to Improve	5 minutes
Apply What You've Learned	30 minutes
Section 3 Contract	5 minutes
TOTAL TIME	**1 hour 15 minutes**

SECTION 1:
MISBEHAVING

Directions:

1) Print your first and last name and date on the spaces provided.

_____

Student's Name   **Date**

2) Read and think about this information.

When you are on the bus, do you misbehave in any of these ways?

- Fighting on the bus
- Getting out of your seat

- Throwing items on the bus
- Bullying others

- Hitting on the bus
- Name calling on the bus

- Yelling out of the window at people passing by the bus.
- Throwing objects out of the bus

THINK ABOUT THESE SITUATIONS:

Do you realize that when you misbehave on the bus that you could get hurt?

If you act up, someone else could get hurt.

If the bus driver is calling you down, is the driver looking at the road or looking at you?

When you are on the school bus, you are on school property.

When you are on school property, the principal can discipline you when you misbehave.

ACTIVITY:
ALISHA'S HURT FEELINGS

Directions:

1) Print your first and last name and date on the spaces provided.

_____

       Student's Name   **Date**

2) Read the story below.

ALISHA'S HURT FEELINGS

Alisha Johnson is in 5th grade. She rides the bus to and from school. Alisha is a good student. Yesterday Robert, a bully, laughed at her about her weight. When she got on the bus the next morning, he called her "fatty". Alisha got out of her seat and told Robert to "shut up". He poked her in the stomach. After that, Alisha had enough and hit Robert in his arm with her pocket book. Robert turned her in to the teacher on duty when he got to school

---

Directions:

Circle the behaviors that Alisha and Robert showed on the bus that you know are not allowed:

        name calling   **teasing**   **out of seat**

   telling someone to shut up   **hitting**   **poking**

   putting other students down   **shouting**   **pushing**

throwing things out of the window

ACTIVITY:
GOOD AND BAD CHOICES

Directions:

1) Print your first and last name and date on the spaces provided.

_____

Student's Name   **Date**

2) Read each situation. In the space provided, write a *G* if you think the statement is a good way to handle a problem on a bus. In the space provided, write a *B* if you think the statement is a bad way to handle a problem on the bus.

....

Example:

> *Situation:* Sam won't let Rodriguez sit by him on the bus ride to school.

____*B*____ Rodriguez hits Sam.

____*G*____ Rodriguez goes and sits by Joe.

....

Situation: Hilda called Ellen "fatty" on the bus.

_____ Ellen fights Hilda.

_____ Ellen talks to the counselor before she fights with Hilda.

Situation: Ramos got out of his seat on the bus. The bus driver had to call him down. The driver hit the brakes and Ramos slid forward.

_____ Ramos is mad at the driver and tells her off.

_____ Ramos realizes that he was wrong to be out of his seat. He apologized.

Situation: Cory stole a pair of shoes from the gym locker room.

_____ He threw them out of the bus window.

_____ Cory turned the shoes in at school and admitted what he had stolen them.

Situation: Alisha is mad at Joseph. Joseph accidentally tripped her yesterday when she got off the bus.

_____ Alisha went to her counselor to talk about being tripped.

_____ Alisha threw a book at Joseph on the bus.

82

ACTIVITY:
THE GROUP

Directions:

1) Print your first and last name and date on the spaces provided.

_____

        Student's Name   **Date**

2) Read this story. Draw a line from the underlined bad behaviors in the story
   to the word MISBEHAVIOR at the bottom.

THE GROUP

Rebecca, Todd and Samantha are good friends. On the bus ride home, they
decided to <u>bully</u> Raphael. Rebecca <u>pinched</u> Raphael. Raphael <u>hit</u> her in the arm.
Todd <u>threw</u> his book bag at Raphael. Raphael <u>stood up</u> on the bus and <u>ran</u> toward
Todd. The bus driver looked in her rear view mirror and saw Raphael <u>out of his
seat</u>. She yelled at him to sit down. He sat down and reported the problem to the
driver when he got off the bus.

MISBEHAVIOR

SECTION 2:
KEEPER SHEET—STEPS TO IMPROVE

Directions:

1) Print your first and last name and date on the spaces provided.

_____

Student's Name   **Date**

2) Read these steps to improve your behavior on a school bus.
   Take this sheet home to help remind you what to do.

STEPS TO IMPROVE

- You need to STAY SEATED on the bus.

- You need to TALK QUIETLY.

- ASK PERMISSION TO MOVE if you need to.

- Keep your hands, legs, books and comments TO YOURSELF.

- SIT BY SOMEONE you can get along with. Ask the driver or your counselor if you may move.

- Take a BOOK TO READ OR A MAGAZINE TO LOOK THROUGH on the ride home. Ask your bus driver if you are not sure if it is okay to bring this item on the bus.

- If needed, ASK THE DRIVER if you can sit behind him/her.

- ASK PERMISSION TO TALK from the driver.

- DO NOT BOTHER other students on the bus.

- REPORT any student(s) who bothers you to the bus driver, counselor, principal or your parents.

ACTIVITY:
APPLY WHAT YOU'VE LEARNED

Directions:
1) Print your first and last name and date on the spaces provided.

_____

        Student's Name   **Date**

2) Look back over the Steps to Improve. Answer these questions.

1. What did you do on the bus to get you assigned to In-School Suspension?

_____

_____

2. Why did you do this?

_____

_____

3. List some of the Steps to Improve that you think might have helped you if you had known or thought about them.

_____

_____

_____

_____

4. Why do you think the Steps to Improve would have helped you behave better? Use the back of this sheet to answer this question if needed.

_____

_____

_____

_____

SECTION 3:
CONTRACT

Directions:
1) Print your first and last name and date on the spaces provided.

_____

Student's Name   **Date**

2) Read this contract carefully. Put a check mark by items you'll work on.
   By signing this contract, you are making a commitment to improve your behavior.

CONTRACT

❑ I will stay seated on the bus.

❑ I will talk quietly.

❑ I will ask permission to move if I need to.

❑ I will keep my hands, legs, books and comments to myself.

❑ I will ask permission to sit by someone I can get along with.

❑ I will bring a book to read or something to do on the bus.

❑ I will ask the driver if I can sit behind him/her.

❑ I will ask permission to speak from the driver.

❑ I will not bother others.

❑ I will report any student(s) who bothers me to the bus driver,
   counselor, principal or my parent.

**I understand that if I do not act better on the bus, that the
principal may take further disciplinary action. I understand that
this packet will be placed in my file to show that the school
has tried to help me improve.**

Write your name in cursive: _____

SECTION 1:
WHAT'S A BUS INFRACTION?

Directions:

1) Print your first and last name and date on the spaces provided.

_____

            Student's Name   **Date**

2) Read the information below.

Do any of these phrases describe you?

> - Fighting on the bus
> - Getting out of your seat
> - Throwing items on the bus
> - Bullying others
> - Hitting on the bus
> - Name calling on the bus
> - Yelling out of the window at people passing by the bus
> - Throwing objects out of the bus

Do you realize that when you misbehave on the bus that you may be endangering your life, the lives of other students and the driver? Many buses hold more than 50 students. Each of those students has a parent or two and maybe even a few brothers or sisters. Have you ever considered how the other students, their parents, brothers or sisters might feel if your misbehavior caused the one they love to get hurt? You are also on school property. This means you can be disciplined for misbehavior on the bus.

You might ask, *"So what if I get kicked off the bus?"* Your parent will have to bring you to school. If your parent cannot, you miss your work, get behind and have to make up the work. Plus you are not getting the benefit of the teacher's instruction. The class is moving on and you are at home. Will it be worth it?

If you are misbehaving just to be cool, consider that your "cool" behavior could cause an accident. Think about how cool it will be if you end up in the hospital or are responsible for others being hurt or worse. That would not be cool at all.

So you need to think about what is and is not proper behavior on a bus. You need to think about this to keep yourself safe as well as others.

On the other hand, if you have a problem, there are people at school who can help. But you've got to ask for help. Maybe your counselor, a teacher, principal, assistant principal or your parent can assist you.

ACTIVITY:
DAMION SHOWS COURAGE

Directions:

1) Print your first and last name and date on the spaces provided.

_____

Student's Name   **Date**

2) Read this story. Then read each situation. Place a check mark by the correct answer.

DAMION SHOWS COURAGE

Damion rides the bus to and from high school each day. Yesterday, Flando shoved him into his seat. The bus driver shouted at Flando to "Stop". Flando stopped. Damion is not a fighter, but he is not a coward either. His father told him that he needs to take care of business by taking up for himself. Damion listened to his father, but he knows his principal and school resource officer have told the students not to fight, but to get an adult involved. Officer Ramos told them that they are not "tattling", just getting help.

Damion knows that his friends on the bus will support him if he fights Flando. However, Damion does not want to get into trouble on the bus. Plus, he wants to get out of 10th grade on time. He has plans to go to college and he does not want this on his record. Damion remained seated. When he got home, he talked to his father. His father went with him to the school the next day to be sure the driver reported the problem. This way Damion was not the reporter.

ACTIVITY:
DAMION SHOWS COURAGE, CONTINUED

Directions:

1) Print your first and last name and date on the spaces provided.

_____

Student's Name   **Date**

2) Answer the questions by placing a check mark by the correct answer.

What is the situation?

❑ Damion had a calm bus ride home.

❑ Damion got shoved by Flando.

Damion listened to his father's advice about taking up for himself.
What did the school resource officer tell the students?

❑ Fight, then call for help.

❑ Back off and don't do anything.

❑ Get an adult involved.

What goal keeps Damion from hitting Flando?

❑ Damion wants to be a prizefighter.

❑ Damion wants to go to college.

❑ Damion wants to have a police record.

What action did Damion take so that the problem was handled?

❑ Damion stood up on the bus and hollered at the driver.

❑ Damion went home and kept his mouth shut.

❑ Damion went home and reported the incident to his father.

ACTIVITY:
JOZETTA ACTS OUT

Directions:

1) Print your first and last name and date on the spaces provided.

_____

       Student's Name   **Date**

2) Read this story. Answer the questions by marking *True* or *False*.

JOZETTA ACTS OUT

Jozetta, a ninth grade student at Middleburg High School, thinks she is bad. The bus driver saw her get out of her seat and walk with shoulders swaggering toward Samantha. Shequila called to Samantha to get ready. Samantha stood up to Jozetta. The students on the bus screamed. Mrs. Jones, the driver, swerved to avoid hitting another car when she told Jozetta to sit down. Everyone on the left side of the bus fell out in the floor. Some of the students were hurt. Mrs. Jones stopped the bus. She picked up her phone and called the police.

True   *False*   Jozetta's walk showed she had an attitude.

True   *False*   Jozetta had permission to get out of her seat.

True   *False*   Samantha stood up to confront Jozetta.

True   *False*   Jozetta was trying to make trouble on the bus.

True   *False*   Jozetta's behavior almost caused a wreck.

True   *False*   All of the students on the bus remained in their seats when the driver swerved.

True   *False*   Mrs. Jones continued on her route without stopping to resolve the problem.

True   *False*   Jozetta's behavior could have gotten many students hurt.

ACTIVITY:
WILLIAM'S PROBLEM

Directions:

1) Print your first and last name and date on the spaces provided.

_____

Student's Name   **Date**

2) Read the story below.

WILLIAM'S PROBLEM

Carla and William have been going together for 3 months. Jessica is a new student. She thinks William is the cutest guy she has ever seen. Last week when William went to his locker, he found a note from Jessica. The note said that she would be saving him a seat on the bus. William talked to Carla and let her know he was going to talk to Jessica on the bus. Carla told William to handle this problem during school and not on the bus.

William decided to wait until he got on the bus to talk to Jessica. When he boarded the bus, Abner was sitting by Jessica. Jessica smiled at William. William tried to sit down by Jessica to explain that he is going with Carla. Abner got mad and told William to "get lost." William tried to explain, but Abner pushed him toward the back of the bus.

ACTIVITY:
WILLIAM'S PROBLEM, CONTINUED

Directions:
1) Print your first and last name and date on the spaces provided.

_____

      Student's Name   **Date**

2) Answer the questions by putting a check mark by the right answer.

Which two students have been going together the longest?

❏ Carla and William

❏ Jessica and Abner

❏ Carla and Abner

❏ Jessica and William

How did Jessica let William know she was interested in him?

❏ Jessica sent word to William by Abner.

❏ Carla told William that Jessica liked him.

❏ Abner told William that Jessica liked him.

❏ Jessica slipped a note in William's locker.

Which place would have been the best place for William to talk to Jessica?

❏ The bus

❏ A private place in school

❏ In the lunchroom

❏ In the halls at school

Which situation could have happened on the bus? More than one can be correct.

❏ A fight could have started between William and Abner.

❏ A fight could have started between Jessica and Carla.

❏ The bus driver's attention could have been taken off the road.

SECTION 2:
KEEPER SHEET—STEPS TO IMPROVE

Directions:

1) Print your first and last name and date on the spaces provided.

_____

       Student's Name   **Date**

2) Read these steps to improve your behavior on a school bus.
Take this sheet home to help remind you what steps you can make to improve.

STEPS TO IMPROVE

- STAY SEATED on the bus.

- TALK QUIETLY.

- ASK PERMISSION TO MOVE if needed.

- Keep your hands, legs, books and comments TO YOURSELF.

- SIT BY SOMEONE you can get along with. Ask your bus driver or counselor if you can move.

- Take a BOOK TO READ OR SOMETHING TO DO on the ride to and from school. Ask your bus driver if you are not sure.

- If needed, ASK THE DRIVER if you can sit behind him/her.

- Ask the driver for PERMISSION TO TALK.

- Ask the driver for PERMISSION TO MOVE, if needed.

- DO NOT BOTHER others.

- REPORT any student(s) who bothers you to the bus driver, counselor, teacher, principal or your parent.

- If a problem starts at school, handle it at school, NOT ON THE BUS.

- If a problem starts at home or in the community, DON'T BRING IT TO SCHOOL. If you don't solve it at home, TALK TO YOUR COUNSELOR.

ACTIVITY:
APPLY WHAT YOU'VE LEARNED

Directions:
1) Print your first and last name and date on the spaces provided.

_____

       Student's Name   ***Date***

2) Write a paragraph about why you are in In-School Suspension. Include the following:
Describe the situation and explain what happened. Then list three steps you will use to improve
your behavior if this situation were to happen again. Use another sheet of paper if needed.

_____

_____

_____

_____

_____

_____

_____

_____

_____

_____

_____

_____

SECTION 3:
CONTRACT

Directions:

1) Print your first and last name and date on the spaces provided.

_____

         Student's Name   **Date**

2) Read this contract carefully. Then put a check mark by items you'll work on.
   By signing this contract, you are making a commitment to improve your behavior.

CONTRACT

❑ **I will stay seated on the bus.**

❑ **I will talk quietly.**

❑ **I will ask permission to move if I need to.**

❑ **I will keep my hands, legs, books and comments to myself.**

❑ **I will ask permission to sit by someone I can get along with.**

❑ **I will bring a book to read or something to do on the bus.**

❑ **I will ask the driver if I can sit behind him/her.**

❑ **I will ask permission to speak from the driver.**

❑ **I will not bother others.**

❑ **I will report any student(s) who bothers me to the bus driver,
    counselor, principal or my parent.**

**I understand that if I do not improve my behavior that the principal may
take further disciplinary action. I understand that this packet will be placed in
my file to show that the school has tried to help me improve the way I act.**

Student's Signature: _____

SECTION 1:
DEFINITION—BUS INFRACTION

Directions:
1) Print your first and last name and date on the spaces provided.

_____

Student's Name	***Date***

2) Read the information below.

Do any of these phrases describe you?

> • Fighting on the bus
> • Getting out of your seat
> • Throwing items on the bus
> • Bullying others
> • Hitting on the bus
> • Name calling on the bus
> • Yelling out of the window at people passing by the bus
> • Throwing objects out of the bus

Do you realize that when you misbehave on the bus that you may be endangering your life, the lives of other students and the driver? Many buses hold more than 50 students. Each of those students has a parent or two and maybe even a few brothers or sisters. Have you ever considered how the other students, their parents brothers or sisters might feel if your misbehavior caused the one they love to get hurt? You are also on school property. This means you can be disciplined for misbehavior on the bus.

You might ask, *"So what if I get kicked off the bus?"* Your parent will have to bring you to school. If your parent cannot, you miss your work, get behind and have to make it up. Plus you are not getting the benefit of the teacher's instruction. The class is moving on, you are at home missing out. Will it be worth it?

If you are misbehaving just to be cool, consider that your "cool" behavior could cause an accident. Think about how cool it will be if you end up in the hospital or are responsible for others being hurt or worse. That would not be cool at all.

So you need to think about what is and is not proper behavior on a bus. You need to think about this to keep you and others safe.

On the other hand, if you have a problem, there are people at school who can help. But you've got to ask for help. Maybe your counselor, a teacher, principal, or assistant principal can assist you.

ACTIVITY:
THEFT

Directions:

1) Print your first and last name and date on the spaces provided.

_____   _____

           Student's Name   *Date*

2) Read the story below.

THEFT

Susan, a 12th grade student, likes to have nice things. On the afternoon bus ride, Susan noticed that Abby had a lot of money in her wallet. Susan decided she would sit by Abby on the way home. Wade thought it was odd that Susan and Abby were sitting together because they were not friends. As the bus left the parking lot, Wade watched Susan look in Abby's purse. The bus took a sharp turn and Wade's attention turned to the road.

The next morning, when Abby boarded the bus, Wade overheard her tell the bus driver that she had some money missing from her wallet. Wade got off the bus and caught up with Abby as they went into the gym. Wade told Abby what he had seen the afternoon before. Abby reported Wade's observations to the assistant principal.

The assistant principal called the director of transportation to ask her to pull the videotape from Abby's bus. Later that afternoon, Abby noted that Susan and School Resource Officer Peyton were on their way to the assistant principal's office. When the assistant principal and the school resource officer showed Susan the videotape, it was clear she had stolen the money. The assistant principal reminded Susan that school rules apply on the bus just like they do at school. The assistant principal recommended Susan for expulsion. If the school board supports this recommendation, Susan will have to repeat the 12th grade.

ACTIVITY:
THEFT, CONTINUED

Directions:

1) Print your first and last name and date on the spaces provided.

_____

      Student's Name   **Date**

2) Answer the questions by circling *True* or *False* for the correct answer.

True   *False*   When students are on the bus; the bus is an extension of the school and the same rules apply.

True   *False*   Susan saw the cash in Abby's wallet. This gave her the idea to steal the money. Plus Susan likes nice things.

True   *False*   Susan stole the money while Abby watched her.

True   *False*   Wade saw Susan steal Abby's money.

True   *False*   Wade reported this incident to the assistant principal.

True   *False*   Abby reported that Susan had stolen her money.

True   *False*   School rules apply on the bus, so the assistant principal could call for the school resource officer.

True   *False*   Since the video clearly showed that Susan stole the money, Susan was recommended for expulsion.

True   *False*   If the school board approves the expulsion, Susan will have to repeat the 12th grade.

ACTIVITY:
DRUGS

Directions:

1) Print your first and last name and date on the spaces provided.

_____

Student's Name   **Date**

2) Read the story below.

DRUGS

Jared, Ronald and Jose were friends whose group was now a gang. They realized that the back seat of the bus was a long way from the view of the bus driver. There were times when Ronald and Jose realized they were living on the edge.

Recently Ronald noticed that Jared often smelled differently in the morning. It was a strange smell unlike any odor Ronald had smelled. Ronald soon realized that Jared was smoking marijuana. Ronald and Jose decided to talk to Jared. Jared told them he was not smoking weed.

The next day as the boys rode home on the back seat of the bus; Jared pulled out a marijuana joint. Ronald now knew what the smell was. Jared lit the cigarette and took a drag from it. The other students on the bus turned around and started shouting at the driver that there were drugs on the bus. The driver pulled off the road and called for the police. When the police boarded the bus, all three boys were taken to the police office. Their parents were called; the school officials recommended expelling Jared, Ronald and Jose.

ACTIVITY:
DRUGS, CONTINUED

Directions:

1) Print your first and last name and date on the spaces provided.

_____

Student's Name   **Date**

2) Write your answers in the space provided.

In your opinion, what is the difference between a group of friends and a gang?

_____

_____

Why do you think Jared lied about smoking marijuana at first?

_____

_____

Would it have been a good idea for Ronald to report Jason as soon as he saw the marijuana joint? Why?

_____

_____

Would the same discipline policy apply to this incident on the bus as if the incident happened at school? Explain why or why not.

_____

_____

Why do you think the police took all three boys to the police department?

_____

_____

ACTIVITY:
OUT OF THE WINDOW

Directions:

1) Print your first and last name and date on the spaces provided.

Student's Name   **Date**

2) Read the story below.

OUT OF THE WINDOW

Allie, a tenth grader at Wausau High School, was in weight training class. Allie's desire to have a newer pair of shoes was getting ready to take a bizarre twist. When Revonda put her new athletic shoes down on the locker room floor, Allie quickly stuck them in a plastic bag and flung them in her locker. Then before leaving for home, she grabbed the bag and ran out to the bus. Once on the bus, the bag was put safely away in her book bag.

On the way home, Allie's conscience began to bother her. She was sitting by the window and began to think about how she could get rid of the evidence. She waited until most of the kids were off the bus. Then, with one toss, out of the window went the bag with the shoes. The driver of the car behind the bus saw the bag come out of the window. This driver stopped and picked up the bag. The car's driver called the school's transportation office and reported the bus number and her location. The driver then took the shoes to the school's principal.

The next day, Revonda realized she had forgotten to put her shoes up. She reported they were missing. Her teacher checked every locker, but Revonda's shoes were not found. Revonda was sent to the principal's office. Upon her arrival and her report, the principal asked her to describe her shoes. Once the description was given, the principal, to Revonda's surprise, produced the shoes.

The principal, who had talked to the bus driver, had narrowed down who was on the bus at the approximate time the car's driver had seen the bag thrown from the bus. The principal checked the class roster for the P.E. class that Revonda and Allie were in. They were the only two female students on the bus. Revonda was charged with theft and misbehavior on the bus. She was recommended for expulsion. Revonda's parents could have charged Allie for theft, but they decided against this action.

ACTIVITY:
OUT OF THE WINDOW, CONTINUED

Directions:

1) Print your first and last name and date on the spaces provided.

_____

       Student's Name   **Date**

2) Put a check mark by the correct answer.

What was the first mistake Allie made?

❏ She stole the shoes and put them in her book bag.

❏ She stuck the stolen shoes in a plastic bag.

❏ She put the stolen shoes in her locker.

Although her conscience bothered her, what decision did she make that was strange or bizarre?

❏ She turned the shoes in to the bus driver.

❏ She turned the shoes in to her principal.

❏ She tossed the bag of shoes out of the bus window.

How did the principal get the shoes?

❏ The bus driver stopped the bus and got the shoes.

❏ Allie asked the driver to stop and she got off the bus and got the shoes.

❏ The driver of the car behind the bus brought them to the principal.

How did the principal figure out which student threw the shoes off the bus?

❏ She compared the list of bus riders with those in Revonda's class.

❏ She viewed the videotape.

❏ She talked to all the students on the bus.

What disciplinary action will Revonda receive?

❏ She was suspended for 10 days.

❏ She was expelled from school.

❏ She was charged and jailed.

SECTION 2:
KEEPER SHEET—STEPS TO IMPROVE

Directions:

1) Print your first and last name and date on the spaces provided.

_____

Student's Name   **Date**

2) Read these steps to improve your behavior on a school bus.
Take this sheet home to help remind you what to do.

STEPS TO IMPROVE

- STAY SEATED on the bus.

- TALK QUIETLY.

- ASK PERMISSION TO MOVE if needed.

- Keep your hands, legs, books and comments TO YOURSELF.

- SIT BY SOMEONE you can get along with. Ask your bus driver
  if you can move.

- Take a BOOK TO READ OR SOMETHING TO DO on the ride
  to and from school. Ask your bus driver if you are not sure.

- If needed, ASK THE DRIVER if you can sit behind him/her.

- Ask the driver for PERMISSION TO TALK..

- Ask the driver for PERMISSION TO MOVE, if needed.

- DO NOT BOTHER others.

- REPORT any student(s) who bothers you to the bus driver, counselor,
  teacher, principal or your parent.

- If a problem starts at school, handle it at school, NOT ON THE BUS.

ACTIVITY:
APPLY WHAT YOU'VE LEARNED

Directions:

1) Print your first and last name and date on the spaces provided.

_____

Student's Name   *Date*

2) Write a paragraph including the following:
   Describe the situation. What did you do? Explain why it happened. List at least 3 steps you could take to improve if this happened again. Use another sheet of paper if needed.

_____

_____

_____

_____

_____

_____

_____

_____

_____

_____

_____

_____

_____

SECTION 3:
CONTRACT

Directions:

1) Print your first and last name and date on the spaces provided.

_____

Student's Name   **Date**

2) Read this contract carefully. Then put a check mark by items you'll work on.
   By signing this contract, you are making a commitment to improve your behavior.

CONTRACT

❑ I will stay seated on the bus.

❑ I will talk quietly.

❑ I will ask permission to move if I need to.

❑ I will keep my hands, legs, books and comments to myself.

❑ I will ask permission to sit by someone I can get along with.

❑ I will bring a book to read or something to do on the bus.

❑ I will ask the driver if I can sit behind him/her.

❑ I will ask permission to speak from the driver.

❑ I will not bother others.

❑ I will report any student(s) who bothers me to the bus driver,
   counselor, principal or my parent.

**I understand that if I do not improve my behavior that the principal may
take further disciplinary action. I understand that this packet will be placed in
my file to show that the school has tried to help me improve.**

Student's Signature: _____

LESSON 5
CLASSROOM/SCHOOL DISRUPTIONS

Grades 4-6

	Title	Suggested Time
Section 1	Disrupting Class	5 minutes
	Building Blocks	15 minutes
	Mr. Cool	15 minutes
	The Class Clown	15 minutes
Section 2	Keeper Sheets - Steps to Improve	5 minutes
	Apply What You've Learned	35 minutes
Section 3	Contract	5 minutes
TOTAL TIME		**1 hour 35 minutes**

Grades 7-9

	Title	Suggested Time
Section 1	Wall of Knowledge	5 minutes
	Ms. Bad	15 minutes
	The Last Straw	15 minutes
	Carey's Actions	15 minutes
Section 2	Keeper Sheet - Steps to Improve	5 minutes
	Apply What You've Learned	35 minutes
Section 3	Contract	5 minutes
TOTAL TIME		**1 hour 35 minutes**

Grades 10-12

	Title	Suggested Time
Section 1	Discipline Record	5 minutes
	Class Clowns	15 minutes
	Late for Class	15 minutes
	Newton's Behavior	15 minutes
Section 2	Keeper Sheet - Steps to Improve	5 minutes
	Apply What You've Learned	35 minutes
Section 3	Contract	5 minutes
TOTAL TIME		**1 hour 35 minutes**

SECTION 1:
DISRUPTING CLASS

Directions:

1) Print your first and last name and date on the spaces provided.

_____

| **Student's Name** | **Date** |

2) Read the information below.

THINK ABOUT IT!

Have you ever thought about why you are in school? Here are some reasons why:

Teachers try to teach you the lessons you need to learn.

This information helps you do well on tests.

The better grades you make, you are more prepared.

The more prepared you are, the better job you can get.

You are in In-School Suspension because you did not behave.

When you misbehave, you do not learn as well.

You keep other students from learning.

These are some reasons that some students do not behave in school:

• Some students need attention.

• Others don't want to do their work.

• Some students have trouble understanding what they read.

• Others have a hard time in math.

• Some students have trouble at home.

• Some students are in trouble at school.

• Some students are trying to be cool.

ACTIVITY:
BUILDING BLOCKS

Directions:

1) Print your first and last name and date on the spaces provided.

_____

        Student's Name   **Date**

2) Read the information below.

BUILDING BLOCKS

When you were little, you might have played with blocks. As you stacked up the blocks, you might have built a wall. You might have tried pulling out one of the blocks to see what would happen to the wall. Well, if you will remember, when you pulled the block out, the wall fell or was not as strong.

Each grade you finish is like a building block. You take the information you learn and add more knowledge to it. From first grade to fourth grade, you learn many things in the areas of reading, math, computer skills, and physical education. When you misbehave, you miss information you may need.

ACTIVITY:
BUILDING BLOCKS, CONTINUED

Directions:

1) Print your first and last name and date on the spaces provided.

Student's Name	Date

2) Read about the lessons this student learned from first grade to fourth grade in grammar and math.

GRADE	GRAMMAR	MATH
1st	alphabet and words	numbers
2nd	words and sentences	adding and subtracting
3rd	sentences and paragraphs	multiplication
4th	paragraphs and compositions	multiplication and division

Directions:

Some spaces are blank. This student misbehaved or was in In-School Suspension when this lesson was taught. Fill in the names of the lessons the student missed from the chart shown above.

GRADE	GRAMMAR	MATH
1st	alphabet and words	
2nd		adding and subtracting
3rd	sentences and paragraphs	multiplication
4th		

ACTIVITY:
MR. COOL

Directions:

1) Print your first and last name and date on the spaces provided.

_____

Student's Name   **Date**

2) Read the story below.

MR. COOL

Brad McGee is cool. All the boys look up to him. He is Mr. Bad. Check out his discipline record below.

Meaning of abbreviations:

ISS = In-School Suspension
OSS = Out of School Suspension

Date	Description— *How he misbehaved*	Subject	Action Taken *by the Principal*
Aug. 15	Throwing paper on bus	Bus	Conference with the student
Aug. 26	Disrespect to teacher	Reading	Conference with the parent
Aug. 30	Did not dress out for class	P. E.	Conference with the parent
Sept. 1	Too much talking	Art	1 day ISS
Sept. 25	Running in the hall	Lunch	2 days in ISS

ACTIVITY:
MR. COOL, CONTINUED

Directions:

1) Print your first and last name and date on the spaces provided.

_____

Student's Name   **Date**

2) From Brad's Discipline Record on the last page, circle the ways that he misbehaved in class or in school.

He threw paper on the bus.

He threw spitballs at his teacher.

He did not dress out for P. E.

He started a fight.

He got out of his seat on the bus.

He laughed at other students.

He was disrespectful to his teacher

He ran through the halls at lunch.

He was unprepared for class.

He was talking too much.

ACTIVITY:
THE CLASS CLOWN

Directions:

1) Print your first and last name and date on the spaces provided.

_____   _____

Student's Name   **Date**

2) Read the story below.

THE CLASS CLOWN

Susan is a class clown. She makes good grades, but cuts up in class. The teacher calls her down, but Susan does not stop. Amy is a good student too. But when Susan acts out in class, Amy has a hard time paying attention.

Amy went to her counselor because of Susan's acting up. The counselor and the teacher worked on a plan to help Susan stop being such a class clown.

The teacher will warn Susan the first time she cuts up. Then she will give Susan lunch detention. Finally, she will call Susan's mother to come and sit with her in class.

When the counselor talked to Susan about the plan, Susan did not want her mom to come to school. She told her counselor she would start behaving.

ACTIVITY:
THE CLASS CLOWN, CONTINUED

Directions:

1) Print your first and last name and date on the spaces provided.

_____

| **Student's Name** | **Date** |

2) Answer these questions by circling True or False.

True   False   *Susan and Amy are both good students.*

True   False   *Susan likes to be the class clown.*

True   False   *Susan's behavior does not bother Amy.*

True   False   *The teacher has not tried to correct Susan.*

True   False   *A plan was set up for Susan.*

True   False   *Susan's grandmother may have to come and sit with her.*

True   False   *Susan wants her mom to come and sit in class with her.*

SECTION 2:
KEEPER SHEET—STEPS TO IMPROVE

Directions:
1) Print your first and last name and date on the spaces provided.

_____

Student's Name   **Date**

2) Read the information below.

STEPS TO IMPROVE

- Ask your counselor, teacher or principal to set up a BEHAVIOR PLAN for you.

- Ask your counselor or teacher to teach you some STUDY SKILLS.

- TALK TO YOUR PARENTS and tell them you need help.

- Tell your counselor, teacher or parent about the THINGS THAT YOU ARE WILLING TO WORK FOR to do better.

- STAY IN YOUR SEAT.

- Learn to RAISE YOUR HAND and wait for your teacher to call on you.

- BE PREPARED for class.

- If you need to be funny, BE FUNNY AT LUNCH OR CANTEEN TIME.

- If you cannot be still or cannot focus, see your COUNSELOR, TEACHER OR PARENT.

- Ask your teacher to let you have a STUDY BUDDY to help you.

- MOVE AWAY from students who bother you.

114

ACTIVITY:
APPLY WHAT YOU'VE LEARNED

Directions:

1) Print your first and last name and date on the spaces provided.

_____

| *Student's Name* | *Date* |

2) Write 4 sentences that tell the following:
- Tell HOW you acted out in class.
- Tell WHY you acted out in class.
- Tell what your teacher or principal did to CORRECT you.
- Look at the **Steps to Improve**. Tell what STEPS YOU WILL TAKE to do better.

Example:

I am in In-School Suspension because I kept getting out of my seat and talking to others. I misbehaved in math class because I didn t understand what the teacher was talking about. My teachers put me in lunch detention and my principal has met with me. I am willing to have a study buddy. I need someone to talk to my mom and dad for me.

_____

_____

_____

_____

_____

_____

_____

_____

SECTION 3:
CONTRACT

Directions:

1) Print your first and last name and date on the spaces provided.

_____

       Student's Name   ***Date***

2) Read this contract carefully. Put a check mark by the steps you will take to improve.
By signing this contract, you agree to work on how you will improve your behavior.

CONTRACT

❑ I will ask my counselor, principal or teacher to set up a behavior plan for me.

❑ I will ask my counselor or teacher to help me work on study skills.

❑ I will talk to my parents and tell them that I need help to behave.

❑ I need someone to talk to my parents for me.

❑ I will stay in my seat.

❑ I will raise my hand to be recognized.

❑ I will be prepared for class.

❑ I will see my counselor, teacher or parent if I am having trouble paying attention in class.

❑ I will ask my teacher for a study buddy to help me.

❑ I will move away from students who bother me.

> **I understand that if I do not stop my behavior that the principal may take further disciplinary action. This packet will be placed in my file to show that the school has tried to help me improve.**

Sign your name in cursive: _____

SECTION 1:
WALL OF KNOWLEDGE

Directions:

1) Print your first and last name and date on the spaces provided.

Student's Name	**Date**

2) Read and follow directions.

> Do you remember learning your multiplication tables? Then you began to learn about fractions, decimals and percents. In other words, what you learned became a base for learning other mathematical information.
>
> As you look at this *Wall of Knowledge* below, think about what would happen if your misbehavior caused you to miss an important fact or an entire lesson.

WALL OF KNOWLEDGE

9th grade	English I or English II	Algebra I or Geometry	Physical Science or Biology I or Chemistry I	World Geography or World History
8th grade	English I or Reading	Algebra I or Prealgebra	Physical Science or Earth Science	American History
7th grade	Reading	Math	Life Science	World Geography

SECTION 1:
WALL OF KNOWLEDGE, CONTINUED

Directions:
1) Print your first and last name and date on the spaces provided.

_____

       Student's Name   **Date**

2) As you look at this student's behavior record, do you see any entries that are similar to how you behave?

> ### Meaning of abbreviations:
> *ISS = In-School Suspension*
> *OSS = Out of School Suspension*
>
> | Date | Description— | Adult in Charge | Action Taken by the Principal |
> |---|---|---|---|
> | Aug. 15 | Throwing things on bus | Mrs. Elam | Off the bus for 3 days |
> | Aug. 26 | Disrespect to teacher | Mrs. Rand | Conference with teacher and student |
> | Aug. 30 | Not doing work in class | Mr. Smith | Conference with Parent |
> | Sept. 1 | Problem for substitute teacher | Mrs. Chassy | 1 day of ISS |
> | Sept. 25 | Unbecoming conduct in hall | Mr. Roberts | 1 day of ISS |
> | Oct. 1 | Unprepared for class | Mrs. Aimes | 2 days of ISS |
> | Oct. 10 | Cutting class | Mrs. Niland | 1 week of ISS |
> | Oct. 15 | Provoking a fight | Mrs. Rand | 1 day of OSS |
> | Oct. 21 | Off limits area | Mr. Smith | 2 days OSS |
> | Oct. 30 | Obscene talking | Mr. Roberts | 5 days of OSS |
> | Nov. 15 | Disrespect | Mrs. Chassy | Recommendation to be expelled from school |

ACTIVITY:
MS. BAD

Directions:

1) Print your first and last name and date on the spaces provided.

_____   _____

Student's Name   **Date**

2) Read the story below.

MS. BAD

Ashley Jamison thinks she is cool. Some of the girls look up to her, others think she is bad. She is a disruption in class. Mrs. Jamison wants Ashley to do better, but Ashley just doesn't see the problem. Check out her discipline record.

Meaning of abbreviations:

ISS = In-School Suspension

OSS = Out of School Suspension

Date	Description—	Adult in Charge	Action Taken by the Principal
Aug. 15	Throwing things on bus	Mrs. Elam	Conference with student
Aug. 26	Disrespect to teacher	Mrs. Rand	Behavior plan by counselor
Aug. 30	Not doing work in class	Mr. Smith	Conference with student
Sept. 1	Problem for substitute teacher	Mrs. Chase	Conference with parent
Sept. 2	Unbecoming conduct in hall	Mr. Rob	1 day ISS
Oct. 1	Unprepared for class	Mrs. Aimes	Study skills taught by counselor
Oct. 10	Cutting class	Mrs. New	1 day ISS
Oct. 15	Provoking a fight	Mrs. Rand	2 days ISS
Oct. 21	Off limits area	Mr. Smith	3 days ISS
Oct. 30	Obscene talking	Mr. Rob	5 days ISS
Nov. 15	Disrespect	Mrs. Chase	1 day OSS
Dec. 11	Disrespect at school dance	Mrs. Jay	5 days OSS
Dec. 13	Threat to school property	Mr. Johns	Expulsion recommended

---

ACTIVITY:
MS. BAD, CONTINUED

Directions:
1) Print your first and last name and date on the spaces provided.

_____

        Student's Name   **Date**

2) Answer these questions after reading "Ms. BAD."

1. How may times has Ashley been written up between August 15th and December 13th?
_____

2. List the different types of behavior Ashley is showing at school and on the bus.
    (Note: You would only list disrespect one time)

    a. _____   *g.* _____

    b. _____   *h.* _____

    c. _____   *i.* _____

    d. _____   *j.* _____

    e. _____   *k.* _____

    f. _____

3. How many different teachers have seen her misbehave? _____

4. List the different interventions her principal has tried.

    a. _____   *e.* _____

    b. _____   *f.* _____

    c. _____   *g.* _____

    d. _____   *h.* _____

5. As you look back over her record on the last page, explain how you know
   her behavior is getting worse.

_____

_____

_____

ACTIVITY:
THE LAST STRAW

Directions:

1) Print your first and last name and date on the spaces provided.

_____

Student's Name   **Date**

2) Read the story below.

THE LAST STRAW

Larry McReed has been disrespectful, cut class, fought others, used foul language, cursed a teacher, and hit a female student in the back. Mrs. Keeper, his principal, has talked with him, had the counselor talk with him, had several conferences with his mom, and assigned him to in school and out of school suspension.

In December, Larry tripped, a student, pushed him into a locker and broke this student's hand. Mrs. Keepers, the principal, has had enough and she is ready to send him to their alternative school. Larry tells his principal that he is ready to go to the alternative school or she can just send him home.

His mom has already promised him that if there were further incidents, she would send him to live with his father in Kentucky.

ACTIVITY:
THE LAST STRAW, CONTINUED

Directions:

1) Print your first and last name and date on the spaces provided.

_____

Student's Name   **Date**

2) Answer the questions after reviewing the story on the last page. Place a check mark by the right answer(s).

Which of the following behaviors has Larry shown at school?
More than one answer may be marked.

❑ Larry has been fighting.

❑ Larry has been spitting.

❑ Larry has been using foul language.

❑ Larry has hurt another student.

What actions has the principal taken?
More than one answer may be marked.

❑ The principal expelled him from school.

❑ The principal talked with his mom.

❑ The principal talked with his dad.

❑ The principal sent Larry to the counselor.

Which of Larry's actions caused the principal to prepare to send him to alternative school?

❑ Larry was disrespectful to her.

❑ Larry called his mom a "dog."

❑ Larry pushed another student into a locker and broke this student's hand.

❑ Larry cut class.

Which statement did Larry's mom make that caused him to want to correct his behavior?

❑ His mom sending him to alternative school.

❑ His mom promising to send him to his father's house.

❑ His mom taking him to counseling.

❑ His mom recommending he be expelled from school.

ACTIVITY:
CAREY'S ACTIONS

Directions:

1) Print your first and last name and date on the spaces provided.

_____

      Student's Name   **Date**

2) Read the story below.

CAREY'S ACTIONS

Arriving at Musgrave High School from the north was going to be a real treat for Carey Hill. She came into school with her sunglasses on, ears and tongue pierced and more holes in her jeans than fabric.

Upon arrival she became friends with Julie Adams. Julie was kind of like Carey, trying to be cool. But Julie was definitely not in the same league as Carey. During the orientation by the high school principal, he reminded the students of general rules and about the drug dogs coming to their school. Then all students reported to class.

Carey and Julie got to be really good friends. They shared lockers, had similar schedules and met everyday for lunch. During second period class, an announcement came on that the school was in a lock down. Carey and Julie knew this was the routine when the drug dogs were in school. However, Julie did not know that Carey was carrying her prescription medicine, Adderal. Carey knew that she was not supposed to have it, so she told her teacher she was sick and had to go to the nurse. The new teacher let her go. On the way to her locker, Carey took the Adderal and slipped it into Julie's locker. Then off to the nurse she went.

About an hour later, Carey passed Julie in the hall. School Resource Officer Payton was taking Julie to the office. Carey just walked by as if nothing was wrong.

123

ACTIVITY:
CAREY'S ACTIONS, CONTINUED

Directions:

1) Print your first and last name and date on the spaces provided.

_____

| Student's Name | Date |

2) Answer the questions by placing a check mark by the correct answer(s).

Which statement would you use to describe Carey Hill?
More than one answer may be marked.

❑ Carey was a typical ninth grade student.

❑ Carey was more hip than most of the 9th grade students.

❑ Carey was trying to be cool.

Why do you think that Julie Adams became friends with Carey Hill?

❑ Carey seemed to be what Julie thought she wanted to be.

❑ Carey seemed like someone Julie would not like.

❑ Carey was a druggie.

Why do you think that Carey dropped her Adderal in Julie Adam's locker?
More than one answer may be marked.

❑ Carey got scared.

❑ Carey did not want to get caught with the prescription drug at school.

❑ Carey wanted to share her drug with Julie.

Why didn't Carey say anything to Julie she saw Julie with the school resource officer?

❑ Carey did not realize what was happening.

❑ Carey was just being a good friend and stayed out of it.

❑ Carey wanted Julie to take the full blame.

SECTION 2:
KEEPER SHEET—STEPS TO IMPROVE

Directions:

1) Print your first and last name and date on the spaces provided.

_____

Student's Name   **Date**

2) Keep this sheet to remind you of these steps you can take to improve.

STEPS TO IMPROVE

- Ask your counselor, teacher or principal to set up a BEHAVIOR PLAN for you.

- Ask your counselor or teacher to teach you some STUDY SKILLS.

- TALK TO YOUR PARENTS and tell them you need help. If you need someone to talk to your parents for you, let your counselor, teacher or principal know.

- Tell your counselor, teacher or parent about the THINGS THAT YOU ARE WILLING TO WORK FOR to do better. These things are called motivators. List them below.

- STAY IN YOUR SEAT.

- Learn to RAISE YOUR HAND and be recognized.

- BE PREPARED for class, use your energy to participate in class instead of disturbing class.

- If you need attention, get your attention AT LUNCH AND/OR CANTEEN TIME, not during class

- If you cannot be still or cannot focus, see your COUNSELOR, TEACHER OR PARENT.

- Ask a fellow student to help you behave. Let your teacher know you are doing this.

- MOVE AWAY from students who may be influencing you to misbehave.

ACTIVITY:
APPLY WHAT YOU'VE LEARNED

Directions:
1) Print your first and last name and date on the spaces provided.

_____

Student's Name   **Date**

2) Write a paragraph that gives information on the following:
- What BEHAVIOR earned you a place in In-School Suspension?
- WHY did you misbehave?
- What INTERVENTIONS has your principal assigned for you.
- What MOTIVATES you?
- What are you willing to do to HELP YOURSELF. (Look at **Steps to Improve**.)

Example:
I am in In-School Suspension because I kept getting out of my seat and talking to others. I think I misbehave in math class because I don't understand what the teacher is talking about. Math has always been hard for me. My teachers put me in lunch detention, my principal has met with me and my mom helps me. Being able to ride horses motivates me. I am willing for a tutor to help me and I could reread my math lesson.

_____

_____

_____

_____

_____

_____

SECTION 3:
CONTRACT

Directions:

1) Print your first and last name and date on the spaces provided.

_____

    Student's Name   **Date**

2) Read this contract carefully. Put a check mark by the items you are willing to work on.
By signing this contract, you are making a commitment to improve your behavior.

CONTRACT

❑ **I will ask my counselor, principal or teacher to set up a behavior plan for me.**

❑ **I will ask my counselor or teacher to help me work on study skills.**

❑ **I will talk to my parents and tell them that I need help to behave.**

❑ **I need someone to talk to my parents for me.**

❑ **I will stay in my seat.**

❑ **I will raise my hand to be recognized.**

❑ **I will be prepared for class.**

❑ **I will see my counselor, teacher or parent if I am having trouble paying attention in class.**

❑ **I will ask my teacher for a study buddy to help me.**

❑ **I will move away from students who bother me.**

Things that motivate me are listed below:

    I understand that if my behavior does not improve, that the principal may take further disciplinary action. This packet will be placed in my file to show that the school has made an effort to present me with steps to help me improve.

Sign your name: _____

SECTION 1:
DISCIPLINE RECORD

Directions:

1) Print your first and last name and date on the spaces provided.

_____

Student's Name   Date

2) Read the information below.

You are supposed to be preparing yourself for the rest of your life. Do you realize what an opportunity you have to take high school courses for the small cost of instructional fees? If you go to college, a book could cost $100. The cost of each course could run from $400 to $650 each. If you take 5 courses each semester, the cost could range from $2000 to $3250 each semester.

Look at Abbie's discipline record. It appears that she may not be interested in completing the twelfth grade.

Meaning of abbreviations:

ISS = In-School Suspension
OSS = Out of School Suspension

Date	Description—	Adult in Charge	Action Taken by the Principal
Aug. 15	Throwing things on bus	Johnson	2 days off the bus
Aug. 26	Disrespect to teacher	Rand	Conference with student
Aug. 30	Not doing work in class	Smith	Conference with the parent
Sept. 1	Problem for substitute teacher	Chassy	1 day ISS
Sept. 25	Unbecoming conduct in hall	Roberts	2 days ISS
Oct. 1	Unprepared for class	Mrs. Aimes	Study skills taught by counselor
Oct. 10	Cutting class	Niland	3 day ISS
Oct. 15	Provoking a fight	Rand	4 days ISS
Oct. 21	Off limits area	Smith	5 days ISS
Oct. 30	Obscene talking	Roberts	1 day OSS
Nov. 15	Disrespect	Chassy	2 days OSS
Dec. 1	Disrespect at school dance	Williams	3 days OSS
Dec. 5	Threat to school property	Johns	Expulsion recommended

ACTIVITY:
CLASS CLOWNS

Directions:

1) Print your first and last name and date on the spaces provided.

Student's Name	**Date**

2) Read the story below.

CLASS CLOWNS

Charles and Jessica are tenth grade students at Seamore High School. Charles wants to be a mechanic and Jessica wants to be a doctor. Both have different plans after high school. Charles, after talking to his counselor, learns that he can attend a technical college after high school. Jessica knows that she will have to attend a four-year college and go to medical school to become a doctor.

Charles loves to work with his hands and school is not very important. He has average grades and does fairly well on standardized tests. Jessica is an overall B student and does not score as well on standardized testing. The problem both of them have is that they love attention from their classmates. They have been known for years as the class clowns. In fact, both have joked that they will be recognized in their high school senior accolades as "Most Likely to Work in the Circus".

Their teachers have tried to talk with them. Lately, Charles and Jessica have been spending a lot of time in In-School Suspension for cutting up. Charles sees that his grades are falling from average to below average. Jessica is now making all average grades.

During a career fair, a mechanic and doctor were present to talk to interested students. The mechanic told Charles that the better his grades are, the less time he would have to spend taking remedial courses at the technical college he plans to attend. The doctor explained to Jessica that average grades will not get her on the path to becoming a doctor. Charles and Jessica are old enough now that they realize that they need to correct their behavior. They decide to put together a plan to help themselves.

ACTIVITY:
CLASS CLOWNS, CONTINUED

Directions:

1) Print your first and last name and date on the spaces provided.

_____

Student's Name   **Date**

2) Answer the questions.

1. **What career goals do Charles and Jessica have and what post-secondary plans (plans after high school) must they achieve to reach their goals?**

   *Charles*_____

   _____

   *Jessica*_____

   _____

2. **Explain the level of work that each student is capable of producing.**

   *Charles*_____

   _____

   *Jessica*_____

   _____

3. **How has the clowning around impacted their grades?**

   *Charles*_____

   _____

   *Jessica*_____

   _____

4. **What type of plan would you recommend to help them?**

   *Charles*_____

   _____

   *Jessica*_____

   _____

ACTIVITY:
LATE FOR CLASS

Directions:

1) Print your first and last name and date on the spaces provided.

_____

Student's Name   **Date**

2) Read the story below.

LATE FOR CLASS

Sam Holmes has finally made it through tenth grade. As he enters 11th grade, he is beginning to think that his high school years are almost over. He likes singing in the concert choir and enjoys running track in the relay races with his other teammates. Sam has not given much thought to his future. He has thought about teaching music or maybe even physical education. He has a B average.

His biggest problem has been getting to class on time. It seems like everyday that he is late to school because his mom does not get him out of bed. Then once he starts off late, he is late to every class. His teachers have talked to him about this. They have told him that it not only disrupts his learning all of the material, but disrupts others when he comes in late. The teachers often have to take time to explain the work. Sometimes, he has to come back during lunch to make up the work he has missed. His girl friend hates this.

The guidance counselor called Sam in and they discussed the problem. The guidance counselor pulled up his record of tardies. His counselor asked him to take the position of an employer, perhaps a principal at a school where he would like to teach. The counselor asked Sam if he would like to hire himself after reviewing his record of tardies?

Sam Holmes' Attendance Record

Date	*Absence/Tardy*	*Reason*	*Excused/Unexcused*
Aug. 30	Tardy	Overslept	Unexcused
Sept. 9	Tardy	Overslept	Unexcused
Sept. 20	Tardy	Dental appointment	Excused
Oct. 1	Tardy	Overslept	Unexcused
Oct. 19	Tardy	Overslept	Unexcused
Oct. 25	Tardy	Doctor's appointment	Excused
Oct. 30	Tardy	Overslept	Unexcused

ACTIVITY:
LATE FOR CLASS, CONTINUED

Directions:

1) Print your first and last name and date on the spaces provided.

Student's Name	Date

After he looked at his record, he said, "This is not good". His counselor asked him what would happen in a work situation if an employee was late to work? Sam said he guessed that others would have to pull his load. His supervisor would have to go over the work assignment with that person. He also might be fired. Then he would have a hard time getting another job, as his supervisor would not recommend him.

The counselor suggested that Sam set an alarm clock and become responsible for himself. Sam agreed to try this. Once he got used to it, Sam arrived at school on time and got to class on time. His grades improved. His girl friend is happier because she gets to see him more at lunch.

Directions:

Read each statement and then circle the correct answer (True or False) from the information in the story.

True   False   Sam has no career goals.

True   False   Sam has a B average.

True   False   Sam would like to be a track star.

True   False   Sam has a problem being absent from school and class.

True   False   Sam's counselor talked with him about his tardies.

True   False   Sam had 5 unexcused tardies during the first 3 months of school.

True   False   Sam's attendance record had a negative impact on his grades.

True   False   The best solution to his problem was for his mom
to pull him out of bed each morning.

True   False   Setting the alarm clock was a good solution for Sam.
He is responsible for himself and is on time to class.

True   False   Letting Sam role-play an employer was a good idea.

True   False   One result of being late for a job might be getting fired.

ACTIVITY:
NEWTON'S BEHAVIOR

Directions:

1) Print your first and last name and date on the spaces provided.

_____

Student's Name   **Date**

2) Read the story below.

NEWTON'S BEHAVIOR

Due to a custody battle, Newton was brought from his mom's home in Australia to live with his father in the United States. Newton is not happy about being here and has thought that he might be able to get kicked out of school. He thinks his father will send him back home after he finishes 11th grade. Check out his discipline record since the first day of school.

Discipline Record

Meaning of abbreviations:

ISS = In-School Suspension
OSS = Out of School Suspension

Date	Description	Adult in Charge	Action Taken by the Principal
Aug. 15	Throwing things on bus	Mrs. Elam	Conference with student
Aug. 26	Disrespect to teacher	Mrs. Rand	Conference with principal
Aug. 30	Disrespect to teacher	Mr. Smith	Parent/Teacher Conference
Sept. 1	Problem for substitute teacher	Mrs. Chase	Conference with principal
Sept. 25	Unbecoming conduct in hall	Mr. Roberts	Parent conference
Oct. 1	Disrespect	Mrs. Aimes	Conference with counselor
Oct. 10	Cutting class	Mrs. Niland	1 day ISS

Newton wants to be a computer assisted design engineer and draw house plans on the computer. Newton went to the school's Career Fair and heard a technical college representative talk about courses in Computer Assisted Design (CAD). Then he went to hear an architect from his community. The architect had gone to technical college to take CAD courses and then went to college to become an architect.

ACTIVITY:
NEWTON'S BEHAVIOR, CONTINUED

Directions:

1) Print your first and last name and date on the spaces provided.

_____

Student's Name   **Date**

> Newton is pretty smart. His overall grade point average at the end of 10th grade was a 3.50. He knows he could do better, but he really misses his mom. He also realizes that maybe his ticket home is to get an education while he has an opportunity. Then he can return home on his own and be prepared to go to work.

Directions:

Answer the questions by placing a check mark by the correct answer.

What is Newton's grade level?

❏ 9th   ❏ 11th

❏ 10th   ❏ 12th

What does Newton want to do when he graduates from high school?

❏ doctor   ❏ architect

❏ computer assisted design engineer   ❏ track star

What are the most frequent discipline problems that Newton has been demonstrating at school?

❏ Disrespect   ❏ Unbecoming conduct

❏ Unprepared   ❏ Problems for substitute teacher

Why is Newton misbehaving?

❏ He misses his mom.   ❏ He likes school.

❏ He thinks if he misbehaves enough   ❏ He likes living with his father.
  he will be sent back to his mom.

What event helped Newton realize that he could work toward achieving his goal?

❏ Meeting with his counselor   ❏ Meeting with his father.

❏ Meeting with representatives   ❏ Meeting with his teachers
  at career fair.

SECTION 2:
KEEPER SHEET—STEPS TO IMPROVE

Directions:
1) Print your first and last name and date on the spaces provided.

_____

Student's Name   **Date**

2) Read the information below.

STEPS TO IMPROVE

- Ask your counselor, teacher or principal to set up a BEHAVIOR PLAN.

- Ask your counselor or teacher to work with you on STUDY SKILLS AND ORGANIZATION.

- TALK TO YOUR PARENTS and tell them you need help to behave.

- Think about what motivates you. In other words, what are you willing to work for? List some motivations here:

- STAY IN YOUR SEAT.

- Learn to RAISE YOUR HAND and be recognized.

- BE PREPARED for class, use your energy to participate in the class instead of disrupting class.

- If you need to be funny, do this AT LUNCH AND/OR CANTEEN TIME, not during class

- If you cannot be still or cannot focus, see your COUNSELOR, TEACHER OR PARENT.

- Ask a fellow student to help you behave. Let your teacher know you are doing this.

ACTIVITY:
APPLY WHAT YOU'VE LEARNED

Directions:

1) Print your first and last name and date on the spaces provided.

_____

Student's Name   **Date**

2) Write a paragraph including the following:
   • Explain the ways you disrupt class or school.
   • Explain why you disrupt class or school.
   • List the interventions your principal has tried to help you correct your behavior.
   • List at least three steps you would be willing to take to improve your behavior.
     Use another sheet of paper if needed.

_____

_____

_____

_____

_____

_____

_____

_____

_____

_____

_____

_____

_____

_____

_____

_____

SECTION 3:
CONTRACT

Directions:
1) Print your first and last name and date on the spaces provided.

_____

      Student's Name   **Date**

2) Read this contract carefully. Put a check mark by the items you are willing to work on.
   By signing this contract, you are making a commitment to improve your behavior.

CONTRACT

❑ I will ask my counselor, principal or teacher to set up a behavior plan.

❑ I will ask my counselor or teacher to help me with study skills.

❑ I will talk to my parents and tell them that I need help to behave.

❑ I need someone to talk to my parents for me.

❑ I will stay in my seat.

❑ I will raise my hand to be recognized.

❑ I will be prepared for class.

❑ I will see my counselor, teacher or parent if I am having trouble paying attention in class.

❑ I will ask my teacher for a study buddy to help me.

❑ I will attend after school study sessions.

❑ I will move away from students who bother me.

Listed below are things that motivate me to do better.

I understand that the principal may take further disciplinary action if my behavior does not correct. This packet will be placed in my file to show that the school has made an effort to present me with steps to help me improve.

Sign your name: _____

LESSON 6
CONFLICT RESOLUTION

Grades 4-6

Title	Suggested Time
Section 1 Conflicts and Resolutions	5 minutes
Conflicts, who can help?	15 minutes
The Best Resolutions	15 minutes
Types of Conflicts	15 minutes
Section 2 Keeper Sheet - Steps to Improve	5 minutes
Apply What You've Learned	10 minutes
Section 3 Contract	5 minutes
TOTAL TIME	**1 hour 10 minutes**

Grades 7-9

Title	Suggested Time
Section 1 Conflicts and Resolutions	10 minutes
Competitive Spirits	15 minutes
Identify the Conflict	15 minutes
Best Resolutions	15 minutes
Section 2 Keeper Sheet - Steps to Improve	5 minutes
Apply What You've Learned	35 minutes
Section 3 Contract	5 minutes
TOTAL TIME	**1 hour 40 minutes**

Grades 10-12

Title	Suggested Time
Section 1 Conflicts and Resolutions	5 minutes
Quarterbacks	15 minutes
Pick a Resolution	15 minutes
College Bound	15 minutes
Section 2 Keeper Sheet - Steps to Improve	5 minutes
Apply What You've Learned	35 minutes
Section 3 Contract	5 minutes
TOTAL TIME	**1 hour 35 minutes**

SECTION 1:
CONFLICTS AND RESOLUTIONS

Directions:

1) Print your first and last name and date on the spaces provided.

_____

Student's Name   **Date**

2) Read the information below about conflicts and solving conflicts.

CONFLICT—

A conflict is when you do not agree with someone else.

Look at these conflicts that you might see at your school or that might have happened to you.

- *Someone else sits in your assigned seat. It makes you mad.*

- *Another student breaks in front of you in the lunch line.
  You don't like this; you were there first.*

- *You don't get picked for the team you want to be on.
  This upsets you because you want to play.*

- *Your best friend tells you that you are not a best friend anymore.
  You can't figure out what is wrong.*

- *Your mom and dad are upset about your grade in spelling.
  You want to do better, but you are having trouble with this subject.*

RESOLUTION—

*A resolution is when the problem
or the disagreement is solved.*

In elementary and middle school, the best way to resolve a conflict or solve the problem, is to get an adult involved to help you. Some students try name-calling and hitting, but these are not good ways to resolve a conflict. Getting one of these adults involved will help.

• Principal	• Parent
• Assistant Principal	• Teacher
• Counselor	• School Nurse

ACTIVITY:
CONFLICTS—WHO CAN HELP?

Directions:

1) Print your first and last name and date on the spaces provided.

_____

Student's Name	**Date**

2) Read the definition of the word conflict. Then read the sentences. If you think the sentence shows a conflict, draw a line from that sentence to the word CONFLICT below.

CONFLICT—
When one student does not agree with another student.

Your best friend shoves you angrily.

Someone tells your teacher that you cheated.

Your brother or sister tells your mom that you hit them and you did not.

Your mother smiles at you.

A student starts a bad rumor about you.

You eat your lunch.

Another student cuts in front of you in the lunch line.

CONFLICT

ACTIVITY:
CONFLICTS—WHO CAN HELP?, CONTINUED

Directions:

1) Print your first and last name and date on the spaces provided.

_____

          Student's Name   **Date**

2) Read the definition of the word Resolution. Place a circle around the names of people who can help you solve a conflict. You may circle more than one.

RESOLUTION—

When the conflict or disagreement is solved, it is resolved.
Resolution means the conflict is solved.

school bully	*assistant principal*	*counselor*
good friend	*younger brother*	*minister*
boyfriend	*teacher*	*nurse*
principal	*parent*	*grandparents*

ACTIVITY:
THE BEST RESOLUTIONS

Directions:

1) Print your first and last name and date on the spaces provided.

_____

        Student's Name   **Date**

2) Read the definitions of the words Conflict and Resolution. Put a *C* in the blank if the situation is a Conflict. Put an *R* in the blank by the Resolution that best solves the conflict.

CONFLICT—
A conflict is when you disagree with someone.

RESOLUTION—
A resolution happens when the conflict is solved.

Example: _C_ Mike and Jeffrey want to be the pitchers for the P. E baseball game.

     _____ Mike lies and tells Mrs. Smith that Jeffrey won't be there for the game.

     _R_ The P. E. teachers gives both boys a chance to show off their skills and then

            she makes the choice.   *(This one is correct because it is the best resolution.)*

- -

     _____ Susan breaks in front of Randy in the lunch line.

     _____ The teacher moves Susan to the back of the line.

     _____ Randy pushes Susan out of the line causing her to fall.

- -

     _____ Homer is a bully. He pushes Jan into her locker. Joe does not like this.

     _____ Joe hits Homer in the face.

     _____ Joe's teacher writes him up on a discipline note.

- -

     _____ Missy tells Melinda that she is prissy pot.

     _____ Melinda takes Missy's pocket book.

     _____ Melinda's counselor meets with both of them.

ACTIVITY:
TYPES OF CONFLICTS

Directions:
1) Print your first and last name and date on the spaces provided.

_____

         Student's Name   **Date**

2) Read the definition of the word Conflict. Draw a line matching the situation with the conflict that fits with it.

CONFLICT—
When one student disagrees with another student.

SITUATION	CONFLICT
Rumor	Susan did not like it when Jamie called her a name.
Horseplay in gym	Don hears Joe spreading a rumor about him.
Bullying	Kristen, a bully, keeps bumping into John in the hall.
Name calling	Chris shoved Ben for the 5th time.
Shoving	Alice threw the basketball and hit Angel in the face again.

ACTIVITY:
TYPES OF CONFLICTS, CONTINUED

Directions:

1) Print your first and last name and date on the spaces provided.

_____

Student's Name   **Date**

2) Read the definition of the word Resolution. Read the resolutions for each situation.
Underline the adult helper who helped to resolve the conflict.

RESOLUTION—
A resolution is when when the conflict is solved.

Example: Susan did not like it when Jamie called her a name. Susan talked to her <u>mom</u> and her mom told her to go to her counselor to get some help. Susan went and she and her <u>counselor</u> talked to Jamie and the name-calling stopped.

1. Don heard that Joe spread a rumor about him. Don went to his teacher.

   His teacher talked to Joe and worked it out.

2. Kristen bumped into John in the hall. John talked to his principal.

   The principal talked with Kristen and the problem stopped.

3. Chris shoved Ben for the 5th time. Chris was ready to fight. His friend, Ray,

   told him to chill out. Chris and Ray saw the counselor for help. The counselor

   talked with Ben and his parent and the problem stopped.

4. Alice threw the basketball and hit Angel in the face again. The P.E. teacher

   saw this and sent her to the principal.

SECTION 2:
KEEPER SHEET—STEPS TO IMPROVE

Directions:

1) Print your first and last name and date on the spaces provided.

Student's Name   **Date**

2) Read the information below. Take this sheet home with you.

STEPS TO CONFLICT RESOLUTION

Stay Cool: Take a few minutes to stop and step away from the conflict. Count to 10 or take a deep breath to help you calm down. Ask your counselor to take you for a walk.

Talk it out: Ask an adult to listen while you talk about the problem. Ask an adult for suggestions. You are not being a tattle tail. You are just looking for ways to solve this disagreement or problem.

Watch your tone of voice: How you talk to the person who is bothering you is important. So be careful how you say what is on your mind.

Body Language: Girls sometimes show attitude by rolling their eyes or flipping their hair. Boys might ball their fist up and shake it at you. These gestures are part of a person's body language. When you are in a conflict or disagreement, be careful of the signs your body gives out. Your teacher or counselor can help you with this.

Privacy is important: If you decide to talk to the person yourself, talk to them in private. Ask an adult to help you find a place you can talk privately. Ask this adult to sit with you in case you need help.

If you need to talk to an adult, tell the adult you need to speak with them in private.

If you are being bullied, do not meet with the bully by yourself. Get an adult to deal with the bully.

ACTIVITY:
APPLY WHAT YOU'VE LEARNED

Directions:

1) Print your first and last name and date on the spaces provided.

_____

            Student's Name   ***Date***

2) Read the conflict and the resolution. Answer the questions by placing a check mark by the correct answer.

Conflict: Allison broke in front of Meg in the lunch line for the fifth time. Meg is about to scream because she left class on time and is the third student in line. Allison is always late. The rules say that Allison needs to get at the back of the line.

Resolution: When Allison broke in line, Meg took a deep breath and went to tell her teacher. The teacher asked Allison and Meg to step into a corner in the cafeteria where there was a little privacy. The teacher told Allison that she would have to get at the back of the line. The conflict was resolved because the teacher handled the problem.

1. What was the conflict?

    ❏ Allison hit Meg in the lunch line.

    ❏ Allison broke in front of Meg in the lunch line.

    ❏ Meg broke in front of Allison in the lunch line.

2. How does the conflict make Meg feel?

    ❏ Meg does not mind Allison breaking in line.

    ❏ Meg is ready to hit Allison.

    ❏ Meg is ready to scream at Allison.

3. How did Meg keep her cool?

    ❏ Meg ran around the lunchroom.

    ❏ Meg counted to 150.

    ❏ Meg took a deep breath and went to an adult.

4. What did the teacher do to help Meg talk the problem out?

    ❏ The teacher took both of them to a private place.

    ❏ The teacher took them to the principal for discipline.

    ❏ The teacher told Meg to just ignore the problem.

SECTION 3:
CONTRACT

Directions:

1) Print your first and last name and date on the spaces provided.

_____

Student's Name   **Date**

2) Read this contract carefully. Put a check mark by the items you are willing to work on. By signing this contract, you are letting us know that you will do the steps you check.

CONTRACT

❑ **I will stay cool by doing at least one of the following:**
Put a check mark by the ways you will try to cool down.

    ❑ **Count to 10.**   ❑ **Talk to my best friend.**

    ❑ **Ask my counselor to take me for a walk.**   ❑ **Get my friend to come with me to talk to an adult.**

❑ **I will talk to one of the following people before I try to resolve the conflict by myself.**

    ❑ **Principal**   ❑ **Teacher**

    ❑ **Assistant Principal**   ❑ **Friend**

    ❑ **Counselor**   ❑ **Other:**

❑ **I will watch the way I talk to the person.**

❑ **I will watch my body language when I talk to the person with whom I am in conflict.**

❑ **I will ask my teacher, counselor or principal to help me find a private place to resolve the conflict.**

❑ **I will not talk to the person who is bullying me without an adult.**

I understand that the principal may take further disciplinary action if my behavior does not improve. I understand that this packet will be placed in my file to show that the school has made an effort to help me improve.

Sign your name: _____

Grades 7-9

SECTION 1:
CONFLICTS AND RESOLUTIONS

Directions:

1) Print your first and last name and date on the spaces provided.

_____

| Student's Name | Date |

2) Read the information below.

CONFLICT—

*When one student or person disagrees
with another, there is a conflict.*

RESOLUTION—

*A resolution happens when the
conflict is solved or resolved.*

Conflicts arise everyday in school and home. Think about some of the conflicts that you see at school.

- *One person does not want another person to sit with him or her.*

- *Two talented athletes try out for the same position on the football team.*

- *There are 7 cheerleading positions open and 25 girls are trying out.*

There are good and bad ways to settle conflicts.

GOOD WAYS TO RESOLVE CONFLICTS:	BAD WAYS TO RESOLVE CONFLICTS:
Get an adult involved.	Fighting
Talk to the other person. *(If the other person is a bully, do not talk directly to them.)*	Getting revenge
Talk in private.	Getting your friends to back you up.
Keep a check on your attitude.	Getting in someone else's face.
Talk calmly.	Talking loudly.
Keep check on your body language.	Making a gesture with your body.

SECTION 1:
CONFLICTS AND RESOLUTIONS, CONTINUED

Directions:
1) Print your first and last name and date on the spaces provided.

_____

       Student's Name   **Date**

2) Read the information below.

STEPS TO SUCCESSFUL CONFLICT RESOLUTION

Stay Cool: As mad as you might be, STAY COOL. Count to 10, take a walk, or talk to a friend.

Talk it out: Talk to the student you are in conflict with. If this does not work, get an adult involved. Don't worry, you are not being a snitch or a tattle-tail, you are just getting some suggestions on how to solve this disagreement.

You can talk to a friend, counselor, teacher, principal or your parent. If someone bullies you, it is not a good idea to talk directly to the bully. Get an adult involved to help you.

Tone of voice: Teenagers tend to show attitude when they are around their friends and peers. Attitude shows up when you get in someone's face or raise your voice. Therefore, when you are working to resolve a conflict, you want to be careful how you say what you say.

Body Language: Body language is shown when you roll your eyes or ball up your fist up at another student. Making gestures with your hand, arm or fingers is also body language. When you are working out a conflict, you want to be careful about the messages your body is sending.

Handle it Privately: If you decide to talk to the person you are in conflict with, do it privately. Think—If you are at school, how many other sets of ears are listening? Also, the other person may have friends who gather around. That can make a difference in the way the other person reacts to you. Think about how unlikely it is that a person will listen, without attitude, when their friends are around? Having friends around as your "back up" can escalate the situation.

ACTIVITY:
COMPETITIVE SPIRITS

Directions:

1) Print your first and last name and date on the spaces provided.

_____

Student's Name   **Date**

2) Read the story below.

COMPETITIVE SPIRITS

Jan and Louise are on the same basketball team. Louise thinks that Jan is always hogging the ball. Louise knows that she needs to run a little faster and work on her dribbling, but she knows she can get better if Jan would just throw her the ball. At the last game, Jan hogged the ball the entire game. After the game, Louise was real upset, so she asked her coach if she could go to her counselor.

The counselor took her on a walk to help her cool down. She also suggested she count to 10. After Louise calmed down, she could talk to her counselor. The counselor told Louise to talk to her P.E. teacher to get some help with running and dribbling.

Louise's P.E. teacher took her and asked Jan into her office. She asked Jan if she would help Louise. Jan agreed. During P.E. the other day, Louise stole the ball from Jan and went to the hoop and nailed a two point shot. With more practice, Jan realized that Louise could be a plus to the team. The conflict eventually resolved itself.

ACTIVITY:
COMPETITIVE SPIRITS, CONTINUED

Directions:
1) Print your first and last name and date on the spaces provided.

_____

    Student's Name   **Date**

2) Answer the questions by placing a check mark by the best answer.

What is the conflict?
- ❏ Jan and Louise are equally talented.
- ❏ Louise wants to be as good as Jan.
- ❏ Jan is a ball hog.

What does Louise do to stay cool?
- ❏ Louise throws the ball at Jan.
- ❏ Louise runs around the gym 10 times.
- ❏ Louise goes to the counselor and they take a walk and talk.

Which adults does Louise talk to so she can get some help?
- ❏ Coach, counselor and P.E. teacher
- ❏ Principal, teacher, counselor
- ❏ Friend, teacher, principal

To which private place did the P.E. teacher choose to take the girls?
- ❏ The principal's office
- ❏ The counselor's office
- ❏ The P.E. teacher's office

Which things did Louise do to help get the conflict resolved?
- ❏ She stayed cool by going to her counselor and taking a walk.
- ❏ She involved other adults.
- ❏ The P.E. teacher handled it privately.

ACTIVITY:
IDENTIFY THE CONFLICT

Directions:

1) Print your first and last name and date on the spaces provided.

_____

Student's Name   **Date**

2) Look at the list of school officials that can help you resolve a disagreement or conflict.
   Underline the situations that show conflicts. If there is no conflict, go to the next situation.
   After you underline the conflict, write down a name of a school official that you could go to for help.

School officials who can help:	
Principal	**Counselor**
Asst. Principal	**Teacher**
Coach	**School Nurse**

Example: Gerald and Harold are best friends, but they are both
going out for quarterback on the football team.

Name of School Official: Coach

• Ternisha and Susan are in eighth grade. They want the same top locker at registration.

Name of School Official: _____

• Henry, Damien and B.J. are all good friends. Henry likes Damien's girlfriend.

Name of School Official: _____

• Ralph and Rodriguez are in lunch line. Ralph breaks in front of Rodriguez.

Name of School Official: _____

• Angel and Marcus are school bullies. They shove James at recess.

Name of School Official: _____

• Maria wrote a note to Danielle. Melissa and Amy roll their eyes at Maria.

Name of School Official: _____

ACTIVITY:
BEST RESOLUTIONS

Directions:

1) Print your first and last name and date on the spaces provided.

_____

Student's Name   **Date**

2) Read each conflict, then read each resolution. Put a check mark by the best resolution.

Henrietta and Beth both like Ben. Ben has written Henrietta that he likes her too. Beth is ready to ask Ben to the school dance.

❏ Henrietta writes Beth a note to keep out of her relationship with Ben.

❏ Henrietta asks her mom to help her think out what to do.

❏ Henrietta decides to fight Beth.

Roberto and Sam are trying out for the school basketball team. Both want to play forward. During a recent practice, Sam sees that Roberto is more skillful in shooting the ball. The coach compliments Sam on guarding other players.

❏ Sam talks to the coach about his skills and considers going out for guard.

❏ Sam challenges Roberto to a shooting match.

❏ Sam quits coming to try outs.

Joining the high school marching band was a great opportunity for Sam and Jennifer. Both students play trombone. Sam wants to be first chair in the band. Jennifer seems to play a little better. Sam notes he is better at the marching.

❏ Sam continues to practice his marching, but does not improve on his technique to play the trombone.

❏ Sam tells Jennifer that her marching is poor.

❏ Sam talks to his band director about how he can improve on his trombone playing techniques.

Rodriguez and Ray want to take a course in agriculture at the career center at the high school. It is time to register for classes. Rodriguez gets his forms in on time and is told he is in the course. Ray waits and turns his forms in late. When schedules are received, Ray is not scheduled in the class.

❏ Rodriguez tells Ray that he is lazy.

❏ Ray decides not to make any further effort to get the semester class.

❏ Ray goes and talks to his counselor to see if he can take the class the next semester.

153

SECTION 2:
KEEPER SHEET—STEPS TO IMPROVE

Directions:

1) Print your first and last name and date on the spaces provided.

_____

             Student's Name   **Date**

2) Read over these steps. Take this sheet home.

STEPS TO SUCCESSFUL CONFLICT RESOLUTION

Stay Cool: Take a few minutes to stop and step away from the conflict. Count to 10 or take a deep breath to help you calm down. Ask your counselor to take you for a walk.

Talk it out: Ask an adult to listen while you talk about the disagreement. Ask them for suggestions. You are not being a tattle tail. You are just looking for ways to solve this disagreement.

Watch your tone of voice: How you talk to the person who is bothering you is important. Be careful how you say what is on your mind.

Body Language: Girls sometimes show attitude by rolling their eyes or flipping their hair. Boys might ball their fist up and shake it at you. These gestures are part of a person's body language. When you are in a conflict, watch the messages your body might be sending. Your teacher or counselor can help you with this.

Privacy is important: If you decide to talk to the person yourself, talk to them in private. Ask an adult to help you find a place you can do this. Ask an adult to sit with you in case you need help.

If you need to talk to an adult, tell the adult you need to speak with them in private.

If you are being bullied, do not meet with the bully by yourself. Get an adult to deal with the bully.

154

ACTIVITY:
APPLY WHAT YOU'VE LEARNED

Directions:
1) Print your first and last name and date on the spaces provided.

_____

Student's Name   **Date**

2) Read the information below about "I" statements and conflicts.

LEARN TO USE "I" STATEMENTS

(Remember, if you are being bullied, always get an adult involved before you talk to them.)

Use "I" statements instead of "You" statements. The person you are talking to will be more willing to listen if you say something like, "I'm feeling angry when you push me in the hall because it made me think you don't like me and I could have gotten hurt." A "You" statement might be, "You pushed me in the hall today and I did not like it one bit. You are a jerk."

Conflict: James has been mad at Joseph all week for writing his girlfriend Amy. James spreads the word that he wants to fight Joseph in the bathroom at lunch. The other students hear about the fight and report it to the counselor. The counselor gets James and Joseph in her office to get them to cool down. After they cool down, they talk about what is bothering each of them. To help them learn to talk to one another, the counselor teaches them about using "I" statements.

Study this format to help you write an "I" statement.

State how you feel:....................James might say, "I was mad

State why you feel this way:....................when you wrote Amy

State how if affected you:....................because I was jealous."

Now think about how much more effective that statement is than James just telling Joseph he is mad at him and wants to fight him.

ACTIVITY:
APPLY WHAT YOU'VE LEARNED, CONTINUED

Directions:
1) Print your first and last name and date on the spaces provided.

_____

        Student's Name   **Date**

2) Write a short paragraph about a conflict you had with someone.
- Explain the situation
- Explain what you did.
- Explain why you reacted like you did.
- Then write an "I" statement that fits your situation.

_____

_____

_____

_____

_____

_____

_____

_____

_____

Use this format to help you write an "I" statement.

    State how you felt: _____

State why you feel this way: _____

  State how if affected you: _____

SECTION 3:
CONTRACT

Directions:

1) Print your first and last name and date on the spaces provided.

_____

Student's Name   **Date**

2) Read this contract carefully. Put a check mark by the items you are willing to work on. By signing this contract, you are making a commitment to work to keep this behavior from happening again.

CONTRACT

❏ **I will stay cool by doing at least one of the following things:**
Put a check mark by the things you will do to stay cool.

    ❏ **Count to 10.**   ❏ **Talk to my best friend.**

    ❏ **Ask my counselor to take me for a walk.**   ❏ **Get my friend to come with me to talk to an adult.**

❏ **I will talk to one of the following people before I try to resolve the conflict by myself.**

    ❏ **Principal**   ❏ **Teacher**

    ❏ **Assistant Principal**   ❏ **Friend**

    ❏ **Counselor**   ❏ **Other:**

❏ **I will watch my tone of voice or the way I talk to the person.**

❏ **I will watch my body language when I talk to the person I am in conflict with.**

❏ **I will ask my teacher, counselor or principal to help me find a private place to resolve the conflict with the other person.**

❏ **I will not talk to the person who is bullying me without an adult.**

I understand that the principal may take further disciplinary action if my behavior does not improve. I understand that this packet will be placed in my file to show that the school has made an effort to help me improve.

Sign your name: _____

SECTION 1:
CONFLICTS AND RESOLUTIONS

Directions:
1) Print your first and last name and date on the spaces provided.

_____

Student's Name   **Date**

2) Read the information below.

CONFLICT—
*When one student or person is upset
with another, there is a conflict.*

RESOLUTION—
Resolution is when the conflict is solved.

Conflicts arise everyday at school and home. Think about some of the conflicts that you see at school.

• *Someone rolls his/her eyes at you. What does that mean?*

• *You get popped by a towel in the gym. Is someone bullying you?
Is someone in conflict with you?*

• *You get a note from the person you are going with telling you it's over.
You aren't ready for it to be over.*

• *Your counselor tells you to get your test registration in on time. It is now overdue.*

There are good and bad ways to settle conflicts.

GOOD WAYS TO RESOLVE CONFLICTS:	BAD WAYS TO RESOLVE CONFLICTS:
Get an adult involved.	Fights.
Talk to the other person. *(If the other person is a bully, do not talk directly to them.)*	Get revenge.
Talk in private.	Get your friends to back you up.
Keep a check on your attitude.	Get in someone else's face.
Talk calmly.	Talk loudly.
Keep check on your body language.	Make an offensive gesture.

SECTION 1:
CONFLICTS AND RESOLUTIONS, CONTINUED

Directions:
1) Print your first and last name and date on the spaces provided.

_____

      Student's Name   **Date**

2) Read the information below.

STEPS TO SUCCESSFUL CONFLICT RESOLUTION

Stay Cool: Take a few minutes to stop and step away from the conflict. Count to 10 or take a deep breath to help you calm down. Ask your counselor to take you for a walk.

Talk it out: Ask an adult to listen while you talk about the disagreement. Ask them for suggestions. You are not being a tattle tail. You are just looking for ways to solve this disagreement.

Watch your tone of voice: How you talk to the person who is bothering you is important. Be careful how you say what is on your mind.

Body Language: Girls sometimes show attitude by rolling their eyes or flipping their hair. Boys might ball their fist up and shake it at you. These gestures are part of a person's body language. When you are in a conflict, watch the messages your body might be sending. Your teacher or counselor can help you with this.

Privacy is important: If you decide to talk to the person yourself, talk to them in private. Ask an adult to help you find a place you can do this. Ask an adult to sit with you in case you need help.

If you need to talk to an adult, tell the adult you need to speak with them in private.

If you are being bullied, do not meet with the bully by yourself. Get an adult to deal with the bully.

Learn to use "I" statements: Use "I" statements instead of "You" statements.

ACTIVITY: QUARTERBACKS

Directions:

1) Print your first and last name and date on the spaces provided.

_____

             Student's Name   **Date**

2) Read the story below.

QUARTERBACKS

Going out for high school sports is a very competitive situation. When two students are athletically inclined and both want to play quarterback; the competitive spirit sometimes causes unsportsmanlike behavior. Ralph and Larry both want to play quarterback with the Jefferson Eagles. Both boys came and worked out during the spring and summer practices. Now it is time for them to show their stuff to their coaches.

Ralph arrives on time, is dressed out and is on the field before Larry drives up. Larry meanders into the gym locker room and gets dressed. By the time he gets onto the practice field, the tryouts have begun. Larry's coach shouts at him to get in line and get going. Larry throws an eye-piercing glance at Ralph. Ralph just shrugs his shoulders and keeps working out.

Larry goes into the locker room and is overheard bad mouthing Ralph. Larry tells the other players what a "jock Ralphy is". Ralph overhears the negative remarks.

ACTIVITY:
QUARTERBACKS, CONTINUED

Directions:

1) Print your first and last name and date on the spaces provided.

_____

Student's Name   **Date**

2) Place a check mark the by correct answer(s).

Ralph showed good effort by doing the following:

❏ Arriving on time.

❏ Shrugging his shoulders at Larry.

❏ Being dressed out and on the practice field on time.

Larry showed poor conduct by doing the following:

❏ Bad-mouthing Ralph.

❏ Coming to spring practice.

❏ Coming to summer practice.

The situation is that there is a conflict over:

❏ Larry wants to be like Ralph.

❏ Ralph wants to be like Larry.

❏ Both wanting to play quarterback.

Was Larry's comment a good or bad resolution to the conflict?

❏ Bad

❏ Good

In the space below, write down how you think this conflict could have been resolved differently.

_____

_____

_____

_____

ACTIVITY:
PICK A RESOLUTION

Directions:

1) Print your first and last name and date on the spaces provided.

_____

       Student's Name   **Date**

2) Read each of these conflicts. Put a check mark by the best resolution.

Abby and Jane like Sam. Abby has been going with Sam for a month. Sam tells Jane he will ask Abby to the dance. Jane wants to ask Sam to the dance.

❑ Jane needs to go ahead and ask Sam to the dance.

❑ Jane needs to back off and let Sam ask Abby since they are going together.

❑ Jane needs to tell Abby that Sam is going to ask her to the dance.

Susan, Ramona, Jessica and Amy run the relay race on the track team. Lately, Susan has been the weak leg of the team. Ramona, Jessica and Amy are trying to decide what to do.

❑ The girls decide to tell her she is off their team.

❑ The girls go to the track coach for advice.

❑ The girls tell Susan she is the weak leg and suggest she get better or she is off the team.

Jason and Starr are going together. Ben is a new student and he has been hanging around Starr's locker. Jason is jealous and wants Ben's attention to stop.

❑ Jason talks with Starr in the counselor's office. Starr tells him she does

    not like Ben. Starr will tell Ben that she and Jason are going together.

❑ Jason confronts Ben. Ben shoves Jason and Jason hits Ben.

❑ Jason asks the counselor to get him and Ben together in her office.

    Jason explains the situation to Ben. Ben tells Jason he likes Starr too.

Ray and John want to attend the local college to play basketball. The deadline for submitting applications is on November 1. John submits his application by October 15. Ray submits his on November 2nd.

❑ Ray's application is late and cannot be submitted.

❑ The counselor tells Ray that the deadline can be extended and he can get it in whenever.

❑ Ray submits the application and pays a late fee.

ACTIVITY:
COLLEGE BOUND

Directions:

1) Print your first and last name and date on the spaces provided.

_____

Student's Name   **Date**

2) Read the story below. Answer the questions by placing a check mark by the best resolution.

COLLEGE BOUND

When John and Jennifer entered ninth grade, they understood that they had to have an average of C or better to be considered for admission to the local four-year college. Since John has been in high school, he is really enjoying the auto mechanics class and he loves to work with his hands. Jennifer is taking some courses in health careers. She is finding that working with medicine may be what she wants to do. She has even considered becoming a doctor. John's parents want him to attend a four-year college. Jennifer's parents do not have the money to send her to a four-year college or medical school.

John wants to learn more about auto mechanics. He may need to attend a two-year technical college. He needs to tell his parents about his plans. Which is the best approach for him to resolve this conflict?

❏ Tell his parents that he is not going to a four-year college.

❏ Ask his counselor to give him an interest inventory and meet

  with his parents about the possibilities.

❏ Go and talk to a counselor at the two-year technical college.

❏ Go to four-year college and forget about his interest.

Jennifer needs financial support for college and possibly medical school.

❏ Jennifer just needs to go to a technical college and be a nurse.

❏ Jennifer needs to talk to her parents and her counselor about her

  desire to go to college and medical school.

❏ Her counselor can point out opportunities for financial aid.

❏ Jennifer needs to work on her grades to be eligible for financial aid of any type.

163

SECTION 2:
KEEPER SHEET—STEPS TO IMPROVE

Directions:

1) Print your first and last name and date on the spaces provided.

_____

Student's Name   **Date**

2) Read the information below. Keep this sheet.

STEPS TO SUCCESSFUL CONFLICT RESOLUTION

Stay Cool: Take a few minutes to stop and step away from the conflict. Count to 10 or take a deep breath to help you calm down. Ask your counselor to take you for a walk.

Talk it out: Ask an adult to listen while you talk about the disagreement. Ask them for suggestions. You are not being a tattle tail. You are just looking for ways to solve this disagreement as a more mature person.

Watch your tone of voice: How you talk to the person who is bothering you is important. Be careful how you say what is on your mind.

Body Language: Girls sometimes show attitude by rolling their eyes or flipping their hair. Boys might ball their fist up and shake it at you. These gestures are part of a person's body language. When you are in a conflict, notice the messages your body might be sending. Your teacher or counselor can help you with this.

Privacy is important: If you decide to talk to the person yourself, talk to them in private. Ask an adult to help you find a place you can do this. Ask an adult to sit with you in case you need help.

If you need to talk to an adult, tell the adult you need to speak with them in private.

If you are being bullied, do not meet with the bully by yourself. Get an adult involved.

ACTIVITY:
APPLY WHAT YOU'VE LEARNED

Directions:
1) Print your first and last name and date on the spaces provided.

_____

Student's Name   **Date**

2) Read the information below on "I" statements.

LEARN TO USE "I" STATEMENTS

Use "I" statements instead of "You" statements. The person you are talking to will be more willing to listen if you say something like, "I'm feeling angry when you push me in the hall because it made me think you don't like me and I could have gotten hurt." A "You" statement might be, "You pushed me in the hall today and I did not like it one bit. You are a jerk."

Situation: Jan and Dean like Amanda. Jan wrote her a note and talked to her over the phone. Dean asked her to go out and she accepted. Deen feels that since he has already asked her out that Jan should back off. Dean told Jan to back off and that he is not married to Amanda.

This format will help you write an "I" statement.

> *State how you feel:*...................Dean might say, "I was mad
>
> *State why you feel this way:*...................when you wrote her a note
>
> *State how if affected you:*...................because I was jealous."

Now think about how much more effective that statement is than Dean telling Jan to back off and that he and Amanda are not married.

165

ACTIVITY:
APPLY WHAT YOU'VE LEARNED, CONTINUED

Directions:

1) Print your first and last name and date on the spaces provided.

_____

Student's Name   **Date**

2) Write a short paragraph about a conflict you have had recently.
- Explain the conflict.
- Explain how you resolved the conflict.
- Explain if this was a successful or unsuccessful resolution. If it was unsuccessful, list some steps you can try to resolve a conflict.
- Write an "I" statement using the format given below.

_____

_____

_____

_____

_____

_____

_____

_____

_____

Use this format to write an "I" statement for your situation.

State how you feel: _____

State why you feel this way: _____

State how if affected you: _____

SECTION 3:
CONTRACT

Directions:

1) Print your first and last name and date on the spaces provided.

_____

         Student's Name   **Date**

2) Read this contract carefully. Put a check mark by the items you are willing to work on. By signing this contract, you are making a commitment to take these steps to improve your behavior.

CONTRACT

❏ I will stay cool by doing at least one of the following things:

    ❏ Count to 10.   ❏ Talk to my best friend.

    ❏ Ask my counselor to   ❏ Get my friend to come with
       take me for a walk.   me to talk to an adult.

❏ I will talk to one of the following people before I try to resolve the conflict by myself.

    ❏ Principal   ❏ Teacher

    ❏ Assistant Principal   ❏ Friend

    ❏ Counselor   ❏ Other:

❏ I will watch my tone of voice or the way I talk to the person.

❏ I will watch my body language when I talk to the person I am in conflict with.

❏ I will ask my teacher, counselor or principal to help me find a private place to resolve the conflict with the other person.

❏ I will not talk to the person who is bullying me without an adult.

❏ I will use "I" statements when I can.

I understand that the principal may take further disciplinary action if my behavior does not improve. I understand that this packet will be placed in my file to show that the school has made an effort to help me improve.

Sign your name: _____

LESSON 7
ORGANIZATION AND STUDY SKILLS

Grades 4-6

	Title	Suggested Time
Section 1	Think About It	15 minutes
	Kate's Grades	15 minutes
	Larry's Luck	15 minutes
	Hosea's Study Habits	15 minutes
Section 2	Steps to Improve	5 minutes
	Keeper Sheet—Apply What You've Learned	35 minutes
Section 3	Contract	5 minutes
TOTAL TIME		**1 hour 45 minutes**

Grades 7-9

ISS Proctor: The arrangement of lessons for grades 7-9 is different. You will select one of the three *Read It* activities: *My Favorite Treat, Going Fishing or Fresh Vegetables.* The student will read sections 1 and 2 and the selected *Read It* activity. Then the student will complete the accompanying *Apply "SQ3R" and Mnemonic Tricks* activity. Finally, the student will complete sections 3 and 4. During *"SQ3R"*, students are asked to quietly recite what they have read

	Title	Suggested Time
Section 1	Avoidance Behavior	15 minutes
Section 2	"SQ3R" and Mnemonic Tricks	20 minutes
	Read It—My Favorite Treat	15 minutes
	Apply "SQ3R" and Mnemonic Tricks— My Favorite Treat	30 minutes
	Read It—Going Fishing	15 minutes
	Apply "SQ3R" and Mnemonic Tricks Going Fishing	30 minutes
	Read It—Fresh Vegetables	15 minutes
	Apply "SQ3R" and Mnemonic Tricks— Fresh Vegetables	30 minutes
Section 3	Keeper Sheet—Steps to Improve	5 minutes
Section 4	Contract	5 minutes
TOTAL TIME		**1 hour 45 minutes**

LESSON 7
ORGANIZATION AND STUDY SKILLS, CONTINUED

Grades 10-12

ISS Proctor: For grades 10-12 you will select one of the three ***Read It*** activities: *Crabbing in the ACE Basin, High School Bound* and *Behind the Wheel*. The student will read sections 1 and 2 and the selected ***Read It*** activity. Then the student will complete the accompanying ***Apply "SQ3R" and Mnemonic Tricks*** activity. Finally, the student will complete sections 3 and 4. During *"SQ3R"*, students are asked to quietly talk to themselves about the information in the story.

	Title	*Suggested*
Section 1	Avoidance Behavior	15 minutes
Section 2	"SQ3R" and Mnemonic Tricks	20 minutes
	Read It—Crabbing in the ACE Basin	15 minutes
	Apply "SQ3R" and Mnemonic Tricks— Crabbing in the ACE Basin	30 minutes
	Read It—Preparing for High School	15 minutes
	Apply "SQ3R" and Mnemonic Tricks— Preparing for High School	30 minutes
	Read It—Behind the Wheel	15 minutes
	Apply "SQ3R" and Mnemonic Tricks— Behind the Wheel	30 minutes
Section 3	Keeper Sheet—Steps to Improve	5 minutes
Section 4	Contract	5 minutes
TOTAL TIME		***1 hour 45 minutes***

SECTION 1:
THINK ABOUT IT

Directions:

1) Print your first and last name and date on the spaces provided.

_____

       Student's Name   **Date**

2) Read about your behavior, homework, studying and organizing.

**Do any of these behaviors remind you of things
you do to keep you from doing your work?
Circle the behaviors that show your habits.**

*I use the bathroom
just to get out of class.*

I lose my homework.

I don't do all my work.

I lie about my work.

*I cheat on tests
and worksheets.*

I don't do homework.

I go see the school nurse even when I am not really sick.

I go see the counselor just to get out of doing my work.

I don't go to class.

SECTION 1:
THINK ABOUT IT, CONTINUED

Directions:

1) Print your first and last name and date on the spaces provided.

_____

        Student's Name   ***Date***

2) Read the information below.

Think about the differences between homework and studying.

Homework:

This is the work your teacher assigns you to do.

> *Example:*
>
> Reading ....Chapter 6..............Read pages 25-32
> Math...............Chapter 7.............Odd numbered problems
> Science...........Chapter 10...........Answer 5 Review Questions on page 110.

Studying:

*This means to read and learn the information
in your book or your notebook.*

Organizing:

*This is how you keep up with all the papers
you receive and the ones you need to return.*

- File or put your papers in the same place all the time.

- Label a folder for Reading, one for Language, another for Math,
  one for Science and another for Social Studies. Then at the end of the day, take
  the folders out and put your papers in them.

- After you finish doing your homework or projects, put your homework in the area
  of your notebook so you will get it back to school. Remember, if the teacher does
  not get it, it can't be graded.

- If it helps, have your parent check behind you everyday.

ACTIVITY: KATE'S GRADES

Directions:

1) Print your first and last name and date on the spaces provided.

_____

Student's Name   **Date**

2) Put a circle around any grades that look like bad grades to you.

Kate Selig's Report Card at the end of 5th grade.							
A = 93-100 B = 86-92 C = 76-85							
D = 70-75 F = 0-69							
Subject	1st 9 weeks	2nd 9 weeks	1st Semester	3rd 9 weeks	4th 9 weeks	2nd Semester	Year
Reading	88	75	81	72	55	64	72
Language Arts or English	97	98	98	90	80	85	92
Math	72	77	75	75	52	64	69

Directions:

Look at Kate's report card above. Use the chart to answer these questions. Put the answers in the space provided.

Answer	*Question*
_____	What is Kate's 1st semester grade in Language Arts or English?
_____	Do you think Kate studied for Language Arts most of the year?
_____	Look at her grades in Reading for the 3rd and 4th nine weeks. How many points did her grade fall between the 3rd and 4th nine weeks? *Remember to use subtraction.* $72 - 55 =$
_____	In math, which nine weeks did Kate make the lowest grade?
_____	Look at the grades in the year column. What subject did Kate make the best grade in at the end of the year?

ACTIVITY:
LARRY'S LUCK

Directions:

1) Print your first and last name and date on the spaces provided.

_____

Student's Name   **Date**

2) Read the story below. Answer the questions by putting a check mark by the best answer.

LARRY'S LUCK

Larry says he is just having bad luck. His teacher writes the homework on the board every day. His school has a homework line. He could call and get his assignments after 4:00 p.m. every day. His teacher also leaves the assignments on the homework line. The problems are that Larry does not write his homework down, he leaves his books at school and he does not study.

What is the reason Larry is not doing well in school?

❏ He writes all his homework down.   ❏ He does not write his homework down.

What isn't Larry getting his homework done?

❏ He leaves his books at school.   ❏ He takes his books home.

Why aren't Larry's grades good?

❏ He studies all the time.   ❏ He does not study.

Why is Larry having bad luck?

❏ He is not lucky.   ❏ He isn't studying and he is not organized.

Read about how Larry can be a better student by being prepared.

❏ Larry needs to write his homework down every day.

❏ If Larry forgets to write his homework down, he needs to call the homework line.

❏ Larry needs to take all of his homework home and do his homework and study.

❏ Larry needs to put his completed homework in a place so he will get it back to school.

ACTIVITY:
HOSEA'S STUDY HABITS

Directions:

1) Print your first and last name and date on the spaces provided.

_____

Student's Name	*Date*

2) Read the story below.

HOSEA'S STUDY HABITS

Hosea is in fifth grade. He hopes he is going to sixth grade next year. His fifth grade teacher has been telling all the students they will have to study more next year. Hosea wants to be a good student, but he does not study.

Here are some study tips his teacher has given him.

- Write your homework down in a homework notebook.

- Take all of your books and notebooks home every night.

- Study for about 20 minutes, and then take a 5-minute break.
  If you need more time, study another 20 minutes.

- Have your parent check over your homework.

- Study and do homework on the subject that is hardest for you first.

ACTIVITY:
HOSEA'S STUDY HABITS, CONTINUED

Directions:

1) Print your first and last name and date on the spaces provided.

_____

Student's Name   Date

2) Read each of the study tips below. Put a circle around the good study skills. Put an X through the bad study skills.

You write your homework down in a homework notebook.

You leave your books at school.

You take your books and notebooks home every night.

You don't study at all.

You do your homework and study for about 20 minutes.
Then you take a 5-minute break.
If you need to study 20 more minutes, then do it.

Have your parent check over your homework.

You forget to take your homework back to school.

You pack your homework that night and take it back to school.

SECTION 2:
KEEPER SHEET—STEPS TO IMPROVE

Directions:
1) Print your first and last name and date on the spaces provided.

_____

Student's Name	**Date**

2) Read the information below.

STEPS TO IMPROVE

- Write down all assignments and homework each day.

- Pay attention to my teacher. Keep my eyes on my teacher.

- Take all books and materials home each day.

- Any work completed at school will be taken home for my parent to see.

- Set aside time to study.

- Do the homework on the subject that is hardest for me first.

- Break up your study time. Spend 20 minutes studying, then take a 5-minute break, then study for another 20 minutes if you need to.

- Do homework first, and then study.

- Study the subjects that are hardest for you first.

- Spend about one hour each day on studying and homework.

- Put my homework in a place to return it to school.

- Ask my parent to help me.

- Ask my counselor or teacher to explain information I need more help with.

ACTIVITY:
APPLY WHAT YOU'VE LEARNED

Directions:

1) Print your first and last name and date on the spaces provided.

_____

      Student's Name   **Date**

2) Answer these questions:

1. How long do you spend completing homework? _____

2. How long do you study and how do you study?

_____

_____

3. What is your hardest subject? _____

4. Why do you think your study habits need to improve?

_____

_____

5. Where do you put your papers you need to take home?

_____

6. Where do you put your papers that you need to bring back to school like signed papers and homework?

_____

7. Look back over Steps to Improve. List at least 3 steps you know that you need to make to improve your grades.

_____

_____

SECTION 3:
CONTRACT

Directions:

1) Print your first and last name and date on the spaces provided.

_____

| **Student's Name** | **Date** |

2) Read this contract. Check off any of the steps you are willing to make.
   By signing this contract, I am entering into a commitment with my principal to improve my behavior.

CONTRACT

❏   I will write down all of my assignments every day.

❏   I will pay attention to my teacher by keeping my eyes on him/her.

❏   I will take all of my books and materials home each day.

❏   If I complete homework at school, I will take it home for my parents to see.

❏   I will set up a time to do my homework and to study.

❏   I will study 20 minutes and take a 5-minute break and then study another 20 minutes if I am not finished.

❏   I will do my homework first and then study.

❏   I will study the subject that is hardest for me first.

❏   I will ask my parent to help me.

❏   I will need someone at school to help me talk to my parents about helping me.

❏   I will ask my teacher to explain things to me that I don't understand.

I understand that if my behavior does not get better, the principal may take further disciplinary action. I understand that this packet will be placed in my file to show that the school has given me information to help me improve.

Write your name in cursive writing _____

SECTION 1:
AVOIDANCE BEHAVIOR

Directions:

1) Print your first and last name and date on the spaces provided.

_____

| Student's Name | Date |

2) Read this information about your behaviors, homework, studying, organizing and "SQ3R."

Do any of these behaviors remind you of behaviors you show to avoid doing your work?

using the bathroom

lying about your work

incomplete work

seeing the counselor

cutting class

loosing your work

seeing the school nurse

cheating on tests

not doing homework

incomplete homework

How you behave in class may cause your grades to be lower than they need to be.

- If you keep yourself organized this will help you keep up with your assignments.

- The sooner you learn how to study and be organized, the better chance you will have at being successful.

- Being able to pay attention helps you listen to your teacher.

- Keeping your eyes on your teacher helps you listen better.

- Writing down your homework everyday and taking the homework notebook home is helpful.

- Taking your books and materials home everyday and going over the material will help you become better prepared.

- Studying 30 minutes to an hour each day will help you learn your lessons.

- Studying an hour during the weekend may also help.

- Reading over the lesson in math and working a few extra problems may help you in that subject.

SECTION 1:
AVOIDANCE BEHAVIOR, CONTINUED

Directions:

1) Print your first and last name and date on the spaces provided.

_____

Student's Name   **Date**

2) Finish reading the information below.

*Have you ever thought about the difference
between completing homework and studying?*

Homework:

This is the work your teacher assigns you to do.

Example:

Reading ....Chapter 6..............Read pages 25-32
Math...............Chapter 7..............Odd numbered problems
Science...........Chapter 10............Answer 5 Review Questions on page 110.

Studying:

*This means to read and learn the information
in your book or your notebook.*

Organizing:

*This is how you keep up with all the papers
you receive and have to return.*

• Filing your papers in folders will help keep things organized.

• Make a folder for Reading, Language, Math, Science and Social Studies. Then at the end
of the day, take the folders out and put your papers that you do not have to return to school
inside of them. Keep these papers until you get your report card.

• After you finish doing your homework or projects, put these papers in the area of your notebook
so you will get it back to school. Remember, if the teacher does not get it, it can't be graded.

• If it helps to have your parent check behind you, ask them to do this everyday.

SECTION 2:
APPLY "SQ3R" AND MNEMONIC TRICKS

Directions:
1) Print your first and last name and date on the spaces provided.

_____

Student's Name   **Date**

2) Read about "SQ3R" below.

"SQ3R"

Learning how to study is very important.
One very effective way to study is called "SQ3R".

"S" STANDS FOR SCAN.

Scanning means to look over the title, subheadings, bold words,
illustrations, photographs and any other information on the page.

"Q" MEANS TO WRITE DOWN QUESTIONS FROM WHAT YOU HAVE SCANNED.

Use words like draw, label, explain, how, why, where, describe, and illustrate
to form your questions. **Example:** Draw a cell. Label the parts of a cell.

"R"—THE FIRST R IN "SQ3R" MEANS TO READ THE MATERIAL ASSIGNED.

Some students like to read the entire assignment.
Others like to break it down into paragraphs or sections.

"R"—THE SECOND R MEANS TO RECALL IT.

Take a few minutes to recite it to yourself outloud. Some students need to
hear what they are saying. Use your own words to help explain it to yourself.

"R"—THE THIRD R MEANS TO REVIEW.

You go back and answer the questions you wrote down and
answer the questions at the end of the section or chapter.

ACTIVITY:
READ IT—MY FAVORITE TREAT

Directions:

1) Print your first and last name and date on the spaces provided.

_____

Student's Name   **Date**

2) Read the story below.

MY FAVORITE TREAT

Flavors of chocolate

Do you have a favorite treat that you just can't do without? Is it one of those things that just makes your mouth water when you think about it? Chocolate does that to me. Think about the different flavors that chocolate comes in. It can be **semi-sweet, dark, milk chocolate and German Chocolate.** It can even taste like mint. German Chocolate makes a great German Chocolate cake with three layers.

Shapes of chocolate

Have you ever thought about the different forms of chocolate? It can be in the form of a Hershey's **kiss, a chip, a bar, or syrup.** There is also chocolate syrup that hardens when it is poured over ice cream. Can you imagine how many chocolate chips you consume when you crunch into a chocolate chip cookie? Chocolate can cover peanuts, caramel and pretzels. It can also be shaped into hearts, bunnies and just about any shape you can imagine.

Where can chocolate be bought?

Chocolate is pretty easy to find. At the grocery store there is an entire aisle just waiting for me. When I check out at the grocery store, there are many of my favorite treats just waiting to be put into the grocery cart. What a selection. Then when I go to the gasoline station, the quick trip to pay for the gas finds me standing in front of the counter with chocolate just within my reach. And if I am lucky, I'll open my kitchen drawer and find a bag that I have stashed away just for me.

ACTIVITY:
APPLY "SQ3R" AND MNEMONIC TRICKS TO MY FAVORITE TREAT

Directions:
1) Print your first and last name and date on the spaces provided.

_____

        Student's Name   **Date**

2) Using the story, **My Favorite Treat**, work through this exercise on "SQ3R".

    1. *Remember the "S" meant to scan what you have read. Write down the phrases or words that were titles, subheadings and/or bold lettered.*

        a. _____   g. _____
        b. _____   h. _____
        c. _____   i. _____
        d. _____   j. _____
        e. _____   k. _____
        f. _____   l. _____

    2. *"Q" means to write questions from what you have scanned. Three questions are provided. Write a question from the remaining 9 items. Use the back of this sheet to write them.*
    (Don't answer these until you go to step 5.)

        a. What are the four flavors?

            1. _____   3. _____
            2. _____   4. _____

        b. What shapes and/or forms does chocolate take?

            1. _____   4. _____
            2. _____   5. _____
            3. _____   6. _____

        c. Why do you think the author thinks chocolate is easy to find?

        _____

        _____

    3. *The first "R" means to read the selection. So now you need to read it.*

    4. *The second "R" means to recite it, aloud, to yourself. So very quietly go through each paragraph and talk about each paragraph's contents.*

    5. *The third "R" means to review. Answer the questions in #2. Use the back of the paper if needed. Remember that you are studying so it is okay to look back over what you have read.*

ACTIVITY:
APPLY "SQ3R" AND MNEMONIC TRICKS TO MY FAVORITE TREAT, CONTINUED

Directions:
1) Print your first and last name and date on the spaces provided.

_____

Student's Name   **Date**

2) Read the information below about mnemonic tricks.

MNEMONIC TRICKS

There are different types of mnemonic tricks (pronounced ne-mon-ik). Mnemonic tricks are ways to help you remember words or lists of words.

A. Using the first letters of each word to form a new word may be one way to remember a list of words. If you take the four words: semi-sweet, dark, milk and German chocolate, you may try to form a new word with the first letter of each word. Since there is no vowel as a starting letter, this is not possible.

If this does not appear to be possible, then take each of the first letters and see if you can arrange them in an order so you can remember them. ***Example:*** SDMG or DGMS. The arrangement you form may help you learn the words.

B. Another trick is to put the words in a specific order. You might want to try to put them in alphabetical order or sequential order (how they appeared in the story). If you have experience with the words, put them in the order of most-liked to least-liked. This ought to be easy since we read about chocolate.

Alphabetical Order	Sequential Order	What I like best to what I like least
dark chocolate	*semi-sweet chocolate*	*milk chocolate*
milk chocolate	*dark chocolate*	*semi-sweet chocolate*
semi-sweet chocolate	*milk chocolate*	*dark chocolate*
sweet chocolate	*German chocolate*	*German chocolate*

C. Another way is to relate the word to something that is familiar to you.

Milk chocolate is my favorite, but I love German Chocolate cake. I'll eat dark chocolate after I have eaten all the other bars in the Hershey's assortment package. Semi-sweet is my least favorite.

ACTIVITY:
READ IT—GOING FISHING

Directions:
1) Print your first and last name and date on the spaces provided.

_____

Student's Name   **Date**

2) Read the story below.

GOING FISHING

Getting Ready

"Hey Josh, Dad is going to take us fishing next Saturday at the coast," Dave said. "Oh boy, I can't wait. We'll get up early and get in the truck and off we'll go. We'll stop and get a sausage biscuit and juice for breakfast," Dave said.

Early Saturday morning, about 4:30 a.m., their dad came and whispered in their ears that they needed to rise and shine. It did not take the usual 15 minutes to get out of bed. Josh and Dave were out of bed in a flash and nearly jumped into their clothes.

When they got downstairs, their mom was already up and had the cooler packed with sandwiches, cookies and drinks for the entire day. As the boys wiped the sleep out of their eyes, they saw that the boat was already hitched up the back of their dad's truck. Fishing rods and reels were mounted in their holders. They were ready to go.

The Ride

Sleeping on the way down to the **South Carolina** coast was the best way for two young boys to tolerate the two-hour ride. But when they were almost to **Edisto Island**, where they would fish in the creeks, the smell of sausage biscuits woke them up. Wolfing down the biscuits and fried potato cakes took only a few minutes. Then breakfast was chased away by a cup of orange juice.

Hooking the Big One

Getting into the boat, they strapped on **life jackets**. These would keep them afloat if they fell out of the boat. The boat slipped into the calm water, the motor roared and they left the dock in their wake. Once they arrived at their dad's favorite fishing hole there was the slippery task of baiting the hooks with the **shrimp**. Live shrimp are feisty little creatures. If you don't hold them just right, well, back into the tidal creeks they go. Once the hooks were baited, the shrimp were cast into the waters of the tidal creek. As the shrimp swam around in the water, they were luring a fish onto the hook. Suddenly, the cork floater on the line took a dive. Dad hollered, "Set the hook, set the hook."

ACTIVITY:
READ IT—GOING FISHING, CONTINUED

Directions:

1) Print your first and last name and date on the spaces provided.

_____

Student's Name   **Date**

2) Finish reading the story below.

Hooking the Big One, continued

The boys knew that meant to pull the tip of the rod up, thereby setting the hook in the fish's mouth. Once the hook was set, they cranked the fish in. Then the fish broke the water, Josh called out, "Did you see that fish?" Then Dave hollered out, "I got one too!" Two **Red Fish**, also called Spot-tails because of the black dots on their tails, were caught at about the same time. What a day!

ACTIVITY:
APPLY "SQ3R" AND MNEMONIC TRICKS TO GOING FISHING

Directions:

1) Print your first and last name and date on the spaces provided.

_____   _____

    Student's Name   **Date**

2) Read and follow directions:

1. *Remember the "S" meant to scan what you have read. Write down the phrases or words that were titles, subheadings and/or bold lettered. There are 9 of them.*

   _____

   _____

   _____

2. *"Q" means to write questions from what you have scanned. Because of the 9 bold items, you need to make up at least 9 questions. Six questions are shown below. Write 3 others on the back of this page.* (Don't answer these until you go to step 5.)

   a. *In general, what was Going Fishing about?*

   _____

   b. *Where were they going to fish?*

   _____

   c. *Once they got to Edisto Island, where would they fish?*

   _____

   d. *What are two important facts from Hooking the Big One?*

   _____

   e. *What kind of fish did they catch?*

   _____

   f. *What is another name for a Red Fish?*

   _____

3. *The first "R" means to read the selection. So now you need to read it.*

4. *The second "R" means to recite or recall it to you. Go through each paragraph and quietly talk about each paragraph's contents. Put it in your own words if you can.*

5. *The third "R" means to review. Answer the questions in #2. Use the back of the paper if needed.*

ACTIVITY:
APPLY "SQ3R" AND MNEMONIC TRICKS TO GOING FISHING, CONTINUED

Directions:

1) Print your first and last name and date on the spaces provided.

_____

       Student's Name   **Date**

2) Read the information below.

MNEMONIC TRICKS

There are different types of mnemonic tricks (pronounced ne-mon-ik).
Mnemonic tricks are ways to help you remember words or lists of words.

A. Using the first letters of each word to form a new word may be one way to remember a list of words. Take the three words life jackets, shrimp and Red Fish.

If this does not appear possible, since there is no vowel starting any of the three words, take each of the first letters and see if you can arrange them in an order to make a way to remember them.

B. Another trick is to put the words in a specific order. You might want to try to put them in alphabetical order or sequential order (the order of how they appeared in the story). If you have experience with the words, put them in the order of most-liked to least-liked. Use these words to do this: life jackets, shrimp and Red Fish.

Alphabetical Order	Sequential Order	What I like best to what I like least

C. Another mnemonic trick is to relate the words to something that is familiar to you.

Write a sentence using these three words: life jackets, shrimp and Red Fish.

_____

_____

_____

188

ACTIVITY:
READ IT—FRESH VEGETABLES

Directions:

1) Print your first and last name and date on the spaces provided.

Student's Name	**Date**

2) Read the story below.

FRESH VEGETABLES

Where do they come from?

Have you ever wondered where the fresh vegetables come from that you see in the display cases of the grocery stores? The vegetables got their start on a farm as a seed or young plant. Did you know that you could grow some of them at your home? These vegetables, **yellow squash, red tomatoes, and bell peppers** can be grown in a home garden. They have a story to tell all by themselves from being a seedling to a mature plant.

Tiller

In the spring, home gardeners begin to prepare the soil for the planting of the seeds or starter plants. Not all dirt or soil is ready for the seeds until it is properly prepared. Many home gardeners have a machine called a **tiller**. This motor-driven soil-rotator has tines. **Tines** are like sharp prongs on a fork. These are the two steps to understanding how the tiller works: The motor turns the tines and the tines turn the soil up from the ground. The seeds or young plants will have good loose dirt to grow their roots.

Planting in Rows

As the soil is turned, fertilizer might be added. **Fertilizer** provides nutrients to help the seeds grow. Once the soil is turned and the nutrients are added, it is time to plant the seeds or plants. Seeds and plants are planted in rows. The reason for this is that it is easier to pick the vegetables. Also, when the weeds begin to grow between the rows, it is easier to pull them up. Weeds will choke out the plant if they are not pulled. Then the soil and seeds are watered. Water is essential for plant growth.

The Final Product

Tending to your plants means that you water them, pull the weeds, and fertilize them. The small vegetables sprout and then grow into mature vegetables. When the plants are **mature vegetables**, you can eat them. That is the best part.

ACTIVITY:
APPLY "SQ3R" AND MNEMONIC TRICKS TO FRESH VEGETABLES

Directions:

1) Print your first and last name and date on the spaces provided.

_____

       Student's Name   **Date**

2) Read and follow directions.

   1. *Remember the "S" meant to scan what you have read.*
      Write down the title, 13 bold lettered words, and phrases.

      _____

      _____

      _____

      _____

   2. *"Q" means to write questions from what you have scanned. Four questions are provided for you.*
      Use the back of this paper to write 9 more questions from the remainder of the bold headings.
      (Don't answer these until you go to step 5.)

      a. What is the story about?

      _____

      _____

      b. What were some of the fresh vegetables that could be grown in a home garden?

      _____

      _____

      c. Define tiller?

      _____

      d. Explain why the season of spring is important?

      _____

      _____

   3. *The first "R" means to read the selection. So now you need to read it.*

   4. *The second "R" means to recite it to yourself. So very quietly go through each paragraph and talk about each paragraph's contents. Put it in your own words.*

   5. *The third "R" means to review. Answer all the questions in #2.*
      Use the back of the paper if needed.

ACTIVITY:
APPLY "SQ3R" AND MNEMONIC TRICKS TO FRESH VEGETABLES, CONTINUED

Directions:
1) Print your first and last name and date on the spaces provided.

_____

Student's Name   **Date**

2) Read and follow directions.

MNEMONIC TRICKS

This word is pronounced ne-mon-ik. Learning a mnemonic trick will help you remember words or lists of words.

A. Making a list is one mnemonic trick. There were two steps involved with the tiller.

List them below. Then when you study, talk through the steps.

1._____

2._____

B. Another trick is to put the words in alphabetical order or sequential order (how they appeared in the story). If you have experience with the words, put them in the order of how you like them, from most-liked to least-liked. Put these words in the order as directed below: peppers, fertilizer, nutrients, home gardeners, spring, tomatoes, squash, tiller.

(*For the third column, only put the vegetables in this story in this order.)

Alphabetical Order	Sequential Order	What I like best to what I like least
1.	1.	1.
2.	2.	2.
3.	3.	3.
4.	4.	
5.	5.	
6.	6.	
7.	7.	
8.	8.	

C. Another mnemonic trick is to relate the word(s) to something that is familiar to you. Try this with the three vegetables: squash, peppers, and tomatoes.

_____

SECTION 3:
KEEPER SHEET—STEPS TO IMPROVE

Directions:
1) Print your first and last name and date on the spaces provided.

_____

        Student's Name   **Date**

2) Read the information below.

STEPS TO IMPROVE

- Write down all assignments and homework each day.

- Take all books and materials home each day.

- Any work completed at school will be taken home for my parent to see.

- Set aside time to study.

- Break my study time up if needed.

- Do homework first, and then study.

- Spend one hour each day on studying and homework.

- Use "SQ3R."

- Use mnemonic tricks.

- Organize your papers each day.

- Ask my counselor or teacher to further explain any information you need more help with.

192

SECTION 4:
CONTRACT

Directions:

1) Print your first and last name and date on the spaces provided.

_____

       Student's Name   **Date**

2) Read this contract. Place a check mark by each step you are willing to take to improve. By signing this contract, you are entering into a commitment with your principal to improve your organization and study skills.

CONTRACT

❏ I will write down all of my assignments and homework each day.

❏ I will take all books and materials home each day.

❏ I will ask my parent to check my completed homework each day.

❏ I will need someone at school to talk to my parent for me.

❏ If I complete homework at school, I will take it home for my parent to see.

❏ I will set aside at least one hour a day to study.

❏ I will divide my study time into 3, twenty-minute blocks of time with a 5-minute break between them.

❏ I will complete my homework first, and then I will study.

❏ I will use "SQ3R"

❏ I will use mnemonic tricks

❏ I will organize my papers each day.

I understand that if I do not take steps to improve my behavior that the principal may take further disciplinary action. I understand that this packet will be placed in my file to show that the school presented me with information to help me improve.

Student's Signature: _____

SECTION 1:
AVOIDANCE BEHAVIOR

Directions:
1) Print your first and last name and date on the spaces provided.

_____

Student's Name   **Date**

2) Read the information below about behaviors, homework and studying.

Do any of these behaviors remind you of how you avoid doing your work?

using the bathroom   *loosing your work*

lying about your work   *seeing the school nurse*

incomplete work   *cheating on tests*

seeing the counselor   *not doing homework*

cutting class   *incomplete homework*

How you behave in class may cause your grades to be lower. Therefore, think about how to get better prepared and more organized. Here are some things to consider:

- The sooner you learn how to study and be organized, the greater chance you will have at being successful.

- Being able to pay attention helps you listen to your teacher.

- Keeping your eyes on your teacher helps you listen better.

- Writing down your homework everyday and taking the homework notebook home is helpful.

- Reviewing the material in your books and notes everyday will help you be better prepared.

- Studying an hour or two, everyday, will help you learn your lessons.

- Studying 30 minutes on Saturdays and/or Sundays may also help.

- Reading over the lesson in math and working a few extra problems may help you in that subject.

SECTION 1:
AVOIDANCE BEHAVIOR, CONTINUED

Directions:

1) Print your first and last name and date on the spaces provided.

_____

Student's Name   **Date**

2) Read the information below.

Have you ever thought about the difference
between completing homework and studying?

Homework:

The assignments given to you at the end of the day.

Example:

Reading ....Finish novel
Math...............Chapter 7..............Odd numbered problems
Science............Chapter 10...........Answer 5 Review Questions on page 110.

Studying:

This means to read and learn the information
in your book or your notebook.

Organizing:

This is how you keep up with all the papers
you receive.

- Filing your papers in folders will help keep things organized. Make a folder for each subject. Then at the end of the day, take the folders out and put your papers that you do not have to return to school inside of them. Keep these papers until you get your report card.

- After you finish doing your homework or projects, put these papers in an area of your notebook so you will get them back to school. Remember, if the teacher does not get it, it can't be graded.

- If it helps to have your parent check behind you, ask them to do this everyday.

SECTION 2:
"SQ3R" AND MNEMONIC TRICKS

Directions:

1) Print your first and last name and date on the spaces provided.

_____   _____

Student's Name   **Date**

2) Read the information below about "SQ3R."

"SQ3R"

"SQ3R" is a very effective study skills method. Learning how to use this study skills method will help you prepare for tests.

"S" STANDS FOR SCAN.

Scanning means to look over the title, subheadings, bold words, illustrations, photographs and any other information on the page.

"Q" MEANS TO WRITE DOWN QUESTIONS FROM WHAT YOU HAVE SCANNED.

As you write questions, use words like these:
Explain, Describe, Define, Illustrate, Draw, What, Why, Where and How.

"R"—THE FIRST R IN "SQ3R" MEANS TO READ THE MATERIAL ASSIGNED.

Some students like to read the entire assignment.
Others like to break it down into paragraphs or sections.

"R"—THE SECOND R MEANS TO RECALL IT.

Take a few minutes to recite it to yourself outloud. Some students need to hear what they are saying. Use your own words to help explain it to yourself.

"R"—THE THIRD R MEANS TO REVIEW.

Answer the questions you wrote down in the "question" part of this method or answer the questions at the end of the section or chapter.

To help you understand how to use this effective study skills method, you will work through this study skills method after reading a story.

ACTIVITY:
CRABBING IN THE ACE BASIN

Directions:

1) Print your first and last name and date on the spaces provided.

_____   _____

Student's Name   **Date**

2) Read the story below.

CRABBING IN THE ACE BASIN

Traveling toward the Atlantic Ocean is an exciting trip. Can you envision the waves rolling in, getting sand in your toes and going swimming in the warm salty water? Along the southeast coastline, there is a city called Beaufort, South Carolina. Near Beaufort, there is an ecosystem called the ACE Basin and there are many **marine** creatures that live in the salt water. One species is the blue crab. Other marine creatures are dolphins, porpoises, sharks and shrimp.

Three Rivers

Near Beaufort, S.C., the **Ashepoo, Combahee and Edisto rivers** converge into Saint Helena Sound to form the **ACE Basin**. The salt water from the ocean and the fresh waters from these three rivers come together and move toward the Atlantic Ocean. As the tides flow in and out, the waters move through the marshes and form tidal creeks. The tidal creeks and marshes support a multitude of marine life such as dolphins, porpoises, sharks, shrimp, and blue crabs.

Places to crab

Many South Carolinians like to go crabbing to catch the delicious blue crabs. One place you can crab is from the banks of the tidal creeks. Another place is from a wooden dock that juts out into the creek. When you find a sandy beach or one where the **ploff** (pronounced fluff) mud and sand mix, you've found a good spot to crab. Ploff mud is a black, thick and slippery mud that lines the bottoms of the tidal creeks.

Equipment

After you've found your spot, you need the proper equipment and bait. A rectangular wooden block, about 1-2 inches wide and six inches long, is the perfect size. Then about 15-20 feet of string needs to be tied and wound around the block of wood. Tie on a small weight to keep the bait on the bottom of the marsh. Finally, tie a chicken leg near the weight. Don't forget a long-handled net and a 5-gallon bucket. You will need the net to get the crab in from the water. Once you've caught the crab you can put him into your bucket that you've filled with the salty water. Are you ready to go crabbing?

197

ACTIVITY:
CRABBING IN THE ACE BASIN, CONTINUED

Directions:

1) Print your first and last name and date on the spaces provided.

_____

Student's Name   **Date**

2) Finish reading the story.

Catching a crab

Once you get to the marsh, stick your net; handle side down, into the sand. Keep it close by you. Fill the bucket with some salty water. Then, with the block of wood in your hand, and the string unwound, toss the string, weight and bait into the water. After the bait sinks, let it sit awhile. When you feel a tug, a crab is gnawing on your bait. Slowly, pull in your string. As the bait and crab come into view, continue to pull the bait toward you, but do not pull it out of the water as the crab will back off and scurry away. Take your net and from behind the crab, scoop him into the net. Then with the crab in the net, take him and turn the net upside down into the bucket of water. Shake the net until the crab drops into the bucket. Remember; do not put your hands or fingers near his claws, because they do bite with their claws.

ACTIVITY:
APPLY "SQ3R" AND MNEMONIC TRICKS TO CRABBING IN THE ACE BASIN

Directions:

1) Print your first and last name and date on the spaces provided.

_____

    Student's Name   **Date**

2) Read and follow directions.

1. *Remember the "S" meant to scan what you have read. Write down the 11 phrases or words that were titles, subheadings and/or bold lettered.*

    _____

    _____

    _____

2. *"Q" means to form questions. Five have been written for you. Use the rest of the words from number 1 to form 6 more questions. Write them on the back of this paper. Wait until you reach #5 below to answer these questions.*

        a. What was Crabbing in the ACE Basin about?

    _____

        b. Define marine.

    _____

        c. What are the names of the 3 rivers?

    _____

        d. What are the best places to crab?

    _____

        e. What is ploff mud?

    _____

3. *The first "R" means to read the selection. So now you need to read it.*

4. *The second "R" means to recite it to yourself. So very quietly go through each paragraph and talk about each paragraph's contents. Put it in your own words if you can.*

5. *The third "R" means to review. Answer the questions from #2. Use the back of this sheet if needed.*

ACTIVITY:
APPLY "SQ3R" AND MNEMONIC TRICKS TO CRABBING IN THE ACE BASIN, CONTINUED

Directions:
1) Print your first and last name and date on the spaces provided.

_____

| Student's Name | Date |

2) Read about mnemonic tricks. Answer these questions to apply information about Mnemonic Tricks.

MNEMONIC TRICKS
This word is pronounced ne-mon-ik. Learning a mnemonic trick will help you remember words or lists of words.

A. One mnemonic trick is to put the words in alphabetical order, sequential order (how they appeared in the story) or if you have experience with the words, in the order of how you like them, from most-liked to least-liked. Put these words in the order as directed below: crabs, dolphins, porpoises, sharks, shrimp.

Alphabetical Order	Sequential Order	What I like best to what I like least

B. Another mnemonic trick is to relate the word(s) to something that is familiar to you. Try writing a sentence with these words to relate them to a past experiences: crabs, dolphins, porpoises, sharks, shrimp.

_____

_____

C. Another trick would be to arrange the first letters of the words in a way to help you remember them. Try several arrangements to see what helps you remember them the best. Use these words to try this: crabs, dolphins, porpoises, sharks, shrimp.

_____

ACTIVITY:
READ IT—PREPARING FOR HIGHER EDUCATION

Directions:
1) Print your first and last name and date on the spaces provided.

Student's Name	**Date**

2) Read the story below.

PREPARING FOR HIGHER EDUCATION

Higher Education and Your Options

Preparing for **higher education** means obtaining further education after high school. While some students will attend colleges, others will go directly into the work force. Colleges prepare you by teaching you information about your major area of interest. Some options you have are listed below.

- Attending a technical college for a degree in a specialty area or to prepare for a four-year college.

- Attending a four-year college to focus on a major area of study.

- Going to work for someone as an **apprentice** to learn a craft or trade.

- Going to work to have a job.

Balancing the Load

As a high school student, preparing to take the next step in life is an anxious time. There are many things to balance. Some students are involved in school athletics; others are involved in high school clubs and organizations. Other students have part-time jobs after school. All students need to be studying to do their best. Then there is the social life. All of this needs to be balanced.

Tests and Daily Work

Getting into a two and/or four year college requires a level of preparation that should include a goal of an overall B average. Students need to take the **Scholastic Aptitude Test** and/or the **American College Test**. Both tests are predictors of how successful a student will be in college. Using your time in class is just one way to prepare yourself for the material on both of these tests. Taking time to study at home and doing your homework is another way to show you can work independently. This also serves to let your teacher know if you understood what was taught that day. Attending review sessions is a great way to learn what is important for you to know for the test.

ACTIVITY:
READ IT—PREPARING FOR... CONTINUED

Directions:

1) Print your first and last name and date on the spaces provided.

_____

Student's Name   **Date**

2) Finish reading the story below.

Identifying Your Interests

There are many ways for students to get information about what they want to do when they finish high school. One of the first things you need to do is to talk to your counselor about taking a **career interest inventory**. These inventories ask you to identify your likes and dislikes. Then they match your likes to career clusters or areas.

Getting Information

Students can attend a school or district **career fair**. A student can make an appointment with a company's human resources department to talk about the opportunities for **employment**, such as a summer job or a part-time job. These give you an opportunity to learn what you like and don't like. Scheduling classes in your area of interest gives you a taste of what is come.

ACTIVITY:
APPLY "SQ3R" AND MNEMONIC TRICKS TO PREPARING FOR HIGHER EDUCATION

Directions:
1) Print your first and last name and date on the spaces provided.

_____

Student's Name   **Date**

2) Complete the "SQ3R" exercise.

1. *Remember the "S" meant to scan what you have read. Write down the 13 phrases or words that were titles, subheadings and/or bold lettered.*

   _____

   _____

   _____

2. *"Q" means to write questions from what you have scanned. Four questions have been written for the 12 items. Write 6 more questions on the back of this sheet.*
   (*Don't answer these until you go to step 5.*)
   a. What is higher education?

   _____

   b. What are some of a student's options?

   _____

   c. What does it mean to Balance the Load?

   _____

   d. What are the SAT and ACT for?

   _____

3. *The first "R" means to read the selection. So now you need to read it.*

4. *The second "R" means to recite it to yourself. So very quietly talk about each paragraph's contents to yourself. Put it in your own words if you can.*

5. *The third "R" means to review. Answer the questions from #2. Use the back of this sheet if needed.*

ACTIVITY:
APPLY "SQ3R" AND MNEMONIC TRICKS
—PREPARING FOR... CONTINUED

Directions:
1) Print your first and last name and date on the spaces provided.

_____

Student's Name   **Date**

2) Read about mnemonic tricks. Answer these questions to apply information about Mnemonic Tricks.

MNEMONIC TRICKS
This word is pronounced ne-mon-ik. Learning a mnemonic trick will help you remember words or lists of words.

A. One mnemonic trick is to put the words in alphabetical order or sequential order (how they appeared in the story). If you have experience with the words, you can put them in the order of how you like them, from most-liked to least-liked. Put these words in the order as directed below: Scholastic Aptitude Test, American College Test, Career Inventory, Career Fair.

Alphabetical Order	Sequential Order	What I like best to what I like least

B. Another mnemonic trick is to relate the word(s) to something that is familiar to you. Try writing a sentence with these words to relate them to one of your past experiences: Career Interest Inventory, Career Fair, Apprentice, Inventory.

_____

_____

C. Another trick would be to arrange the first letters of the words in a way to help you remember them. Try several arrangements to see what helps you remember them the best. Use these words to try this: Career Interest Inventory, Career Fair, Apprentice, Inventory

_____

ACTIVITY:
READ IT—BEHIND THE WHEEL

Directions:

1) Print your first and last name and date on the spaces provided.

_____

       Student's Name   **Date**

2) Read the story below.

BEHIND THE WHEEL

Maturity and Responsibility

There is nothing in the world that can match the desire to drive. Just to get behind the wheel of an automated machine, put it in gear, and press the accelerator is a thrill! Being able to drive represents maturity and responsibility. This means your parents think you are grown up enough to take care of the car, yourself and others on the road. Consider that you are behind the wheel of a car or truck that costs thousands of dollars. Besides that it can go in excess of 100 miles per hour. On top of that it weighs thousands of pounds and if misused can do damage to you and someone else.

Rules of the Road

One of the first things teenagers learn as they prepare to learn to drive is that there are rules and insurance. When you buy **insurance** you enter into a contract to pay an insurance company a **premium** or payment. In turn, they agree to cover you with **liability** and **collision insurance**. Liability insurance means that if you hurt someone in a wreck or accident, that the insurance company will pay the other driver and passengers for their injuries. Collision insurance means that if their vehicle or your vehicle gets damaged, that the damage can be fixed and paid for.

Your parent may want you to pay for gas as well as for your insurance premium. Getting a part-time job helps to ensure that the insurance costs will be paid.

Fueling the Ride

Having your parent's credit card makes buying gasoline less of a shock. However, if your parent gives you the responsibility of paying for your own gasoline, then a full tank may cost more than you have in your wallet. This makes joy riding much less of a joy.

ACTIVITY:
APPLY "SQ3R" AND MNEMONIC TRICKS—BEHIND THE WHEEL

Directions:

1) Print your first and last name and date on the spaces provided.

_____

        Student's Name   **Date**

2) Read and follow directions.

1. *Remember the "S" meant to scan what you have read. Write down the 8 phrases or words that were titles, subheadings and/or bold lettered.*

   _____

   _____

   _____

2. *"Q" means to write questions from what you have scanned. Four questions have been written for you. Write 4 more questions on the back of this sheet.*

   (Don't answer these until you go to step 5.)

   a. Define maturity.

   _____

   b. Define responsibility.

   _____

   c. Explain insurance.

   _____

   d. Explain the difference between collision and liability insurance.

   _____

   _____

3. *The first "R" means to read the selection. So now you need to read it.*

4. *The second "R" means to recite it to yourself. So very quietly talk to yourself about what you read. Put it in your own words if you can.*

5. *The third "R" means to review. Answer the questions from #2. Use the back of this sheet if needed.*

ACTIVITY:
APPLY "SQ3R" AND MNEMONIC TRICKS—
BEHIND THE WHEEL, CONTINUED

Directions:
1) Print your first and last name and date on the spaces provided.

_____   _____

Student's Name   **Date**

2) Read the information below about mnemonic tricks.

MNEMONIC TRICKS
This word is pronounced ne-mon-ik. Learning a mnemonic trick will help you remember words or lists of words.

A. One mnemonic trick is to put the words in alphabetical order or sequential order (how they appeared in the story). If you have experience with the words, you can put them in the order of how you like them, from most-liked to least-liked. Put these words in the order as directed below: maturity, responsibility, insurance, premium, liability, collision.

Alphabetical Order	Sequential Order	What I like best to what I like least

B. Another mnemonic trick is to relate the word(s) to something that is familiar to you. Try writing a sentence with these words to relate them to an experience: maturity, responsibility, insurance, collision.

_____

_____

C. Another trick would be to arrange the first letters of the words in a way to help you remember them. Try several arrangements to see what helps you remember them the best. Use these words to try this: maturity, responsibility, insurance, premium, liability, collision.

_____

_____

SECTION 3:
KEEPER SHEET—STEPS TO IMPROVE

Directions:

1) Print your first and last name and date on the spaces provided.

_____

Student's Name   **Date**

2) Read the information below.

STEPS TO IMPROVE

- Write down all assignments and homework each day.

- Take all books and materials home each day.

- Any work completed at school will be taken home for my parent to see.

- Set aside one to two hours to study Monday through Friday. Set aside an hour or two during the weekend to study.

- Break up your study time up if needed.

- Do homework first, and then study.

- Use "SQ3R."

- Use mnemonic tricks.

- Organize your papers each day.

- Ask my counselor or teacher to further explain any information you need more help with.

- Attend study or review sessions if possible.

SECTION 4:
CONTRACT

Directions:

1) Print your first and last name and date on the spaces provided.

_____

        Student's Name   ***Date***

2) Read this contract. Place a check mark by each step you are willing to take to improve. By signing this contract, you are entering into a commitment with your principal to improve your organization and study skills.

CONTRACT

❑ I will write down all of my assignments and homework each day.

❑ I will take all books and materials home each day.

❑ I will ask my parent to check my completed homework each day.

❑ If I complete homework at school, I will take it home for my parent to see.

❑ I will set aside time to study during the week and weekends.

❑ I will break up my study time, if needed.

❑ I will complete my homework first, and then I will study.

❑ I will spend one to two hours each day to study and complete homework.

❑ I will use "SQ3R".

❑ I will use mnemonic tricks.

❑ I will organize my papers each day.

❑ I will attend study or review sessions, if possible.

I understand that if I do not take steps to improve my behavior that the principal may take further disciplinary action. I understand that this packet will be placed in my file to show that the school presented me with information to help me improve.

Student's Signature: _____

REFERENCES

Henson, Shea (2002). Wooly Bully: Bullying Prevention in Elementary and Middle Schools: Simpsonville, SC.

Langan, Paul (2004). Bullying in Schools. What you need to know. Townsend Press, 9.

Lifetime Learning Systems, Inc. (2001). Right Decision, Right Now. Issue: Reacting to Conflict. Activity four.

ABOUT THE AUTHOR

Catherine H. Pardue is a guidance counselor and licensed professional counselor in a middle school setting in South Carolina. She received her Bachelor of Arts in Psychology and Masters in Education in Secondary School Guidance and Counseling from the University of South Carolina. As an educator in South Carolina, her certification is a Masters plus 30 hours. She has more than 17 years of experience working with students, parents, teachers and administrators from kindergarten through high school. She has been instrumental in developing and implementing a Life Skills course for eighth grade students, a program in career awareness and exploration and a business partnership program in her current setting. Mrs. Pardue initiated the unique format for her county's career fair. She has been a co-presenter at the South Carolina Middle School's Conference and at the S.C. Business and Education Summit.